MW00886926

A PROVERB A DAY

40-Day Devotional

SARAH J CALLEN

A PROVERB A DAY

Copyright © 2019 by Sarah J Callen

Hardcover ISBN: 9798717406628
Paperback ISBN: 9781794198494
ASIN: B07NCDNC37

2019—First Edition

Printed in the United States of America

Edited by Amy A. Noelck

Cover designed by Sarah J Callen
Cover art by Cynthia Arenado

CONTENTS

INTRODUCTION: A PROVERB A DAY

I'm so happy you've picked up this book! I hope it encourages, inspires, and challenges you as you make your way through each page. But before we dive in, let's go over two important things I want you to keep in mind as you read:

1. Slowness over speed.

2. Wisdom is an open invitation.

Go Slow

This book is meant to be read slowly. Our lives are filled with busyness, color-coded schedules, and far too many appointments. Right now, I'm writing this while on a plane, flying from my home to my current 9-5 job—trust me, I get the whole hectic schedule thing. Amidst the busyness, there's so much to be gained from a few intentional moments of slowness.

As you may have noticed, this is a 40-day devotional, but there are only 31 Proverbs. This doesn't mean that we're going to be sitting around, twiddling our thumbs for the other nine days (at least I hope not). Instead, we're going to dig into some of the individual Proverbs a little deeper—some of them spanning multiple days.

I encourage you to do this for yourself. If there's a particular day or Proverb that stands out to you, focus on it for an extra day or a whole week. It won't bother me. This is your study, and you can tailor it to suit your needs. I'm in no rush. If on Day 20 you feel like you need to return to something from Day 4—go for it!

There's no time limit here. There's no race to finish. This is just a sweet invitation to spend time with the One who loves you dearly.

Just Ask

The book of James is an excellent complement to Proverbs. It's amazing how these two men, decades and many miles apart, could be on the same page!

In James 1, the author encourages the reader to ask for wisdom if they feel like they're lacking. There are no rules or stipulations or requirements to get wisdom, other than realizing you need it and asking the One who gives wisdom abundantly. This is exactly what Solomon did. He asked God for wisdom and God graciously granted it to him.

I believe that God wants to do the same thing for us. I think, over the course of this book, as we're seeking God's face and asking Him for wisdom, He will give to us abundantly!

Now, let's dive in!

DAY 1: A BACKSTORY

What do you hope to gain by the end of this study?

Before diving into any book, I believe it's a good idea to do some research and learn the who, when, and why of the text. As we do that, we'll learn some important truths along the way!

So, without further ado, let's dive in!

Who Wrote It?

Proverbs is primarily attributed to Solomon because his name is in the first chapter and references are made to him throughout the book. But he didn't write this book alone. Some sections were written by a group of wise men, Agur (son of Jakeh), and a man named King Lemuel. Proverbs was also edited and added to by a group of scribes who helped shape the words we have in front of us today.

This might seem like a small detail, but I love what it teaches us about the nature of the church and the body of Christ (though they didn't use those terms when Proverbs was written). These wise and God-fearing men each used their gifts so we could learn more about who God is, who we are, and how we're called to live! This reminds me that, no matter our skill sets, we each have something to add to the Kingdom!

When Was It Written?

Solomon ruled in the 10th century B.C., a prosperous time for the nation when copious amounts of literature were being produced. People were seeking after God and praising Him for the many blessings He had showered upon the country. But then, following the pattern of previous generations, they began worshipping other gods, and things went sideways.

Then, a few hundred years later, these wise writings were resurrected and edited as spiritual revival swept through the nation under King Hezekiah's rule. The people who had been without God for so long craved wisdom, truth, and took the time to seek His face.

Their compilation, resurrection, and renewal of this text remind me that nothing done for God is ever wasted. We have the words of Proverbs in front of us today as a result of Hezekiah's love for God and the scribes' devotion. I wonder if these faithful men understood the widespread ramifications their actions would have. The roles we play now might seem minute or insignificant, but we don't know the ripple effects they may cause.

What's The Point?

Proverbs is a collection of many short phrases that explain general truths about human behavior. These phrases aren't promises or prophecies but are generalities about how things tend to work. There are no guarantees in the book of Proverbs — it's not that kind of book.

It goes beyond good advice and touches on some incredibly practical advice for the readers. There are warnings against lying, stealing, and slothfulness. People are instructed to treat each other well and run from evil when they spot it. Readers are encouraged to pursue God passionately and heed His Word because what He gives, gives life.

While there are many good lessons, the one that stands out to me most is that God is after our hearts.

Throughout Proverbs, we're reminded of how important our affections are and how they influence everything we do. So, if we fear, love, and desire God, He will capture our hearts, and all of the behavior modification recommendations contained in the book will flow as a result of our heart changes. But it all starts with the heart.

I'm thrilled to be diving into these wisdom-filled chapters with you over the coming weeks. I know this is going to be a time of growth, learning, and heart-change for each of us as we go through this study. As I was writing this, I was encouraged to go deeper in my relationship with God—who loves me more than I can comprehend—and I hope you experience the same!

Reflection

Do you believe what you do in the world matters? Why or why not?

Do = action

Yes, what I do matters. Each choice, word, act has an effect on not only me, but the world around me & most importantly other people. God gives us the choice to lift up or tear down in all circumstances.

Do you believe God wants your heart? Why or why not?

Yes, God wants my heart. He wants & knows what is best for me and everything begins in the heart. Out of it flows everything. So if He has my heart, he will grow me into the woman that he created me to be. I can trust Him with my heart. He will be delicate with it and not take lightly the responsibility of caring for it. He wants a relationship with us!

What is God saying to you?

Seek My words for wisdom

Do = action - Engage in acquiring
wisdom - It takes
self discipline

Proverbs is a simple invitation to
grow... Not to feel guilt about
the ways you've done wrong.

My heavenly Father <u>wants</u> a
relationship with me.

DAY 2: PROVERBS 1

Read Proverbs Chapter 1.

What stood out to you in today's Proverb?

Verse 10:
   If sinners entice you, turn your
   back on them.

-Don't go along with them, stay far
   away from their paths

But all who listen to me will live in
      peace.

                              What do I
                              -Value
                              -Cherish
Core Value Activity   -Pursue

7

I once did a core value exercise with a group of people and was blown away by the results. Each of us picked five words that meant the most to us from about 30 options. As we discussed, I was amazed and thankful for how different our responses were—we are all so unique and varied!

Though intelligence, knowledge, and learning were all on the list, I chose wisdom as one of my values because I see wisdom as the application of knowledge. I never want to know something and then do nothing with it. I want to be wise and have expertise in action.

Solomon starts us off with a challenge to gain wisdom and knowledge—both of which originate with God and set the stage for the rest of the book. Here, he lays out just what his aim is and precisely what we can expect as we read further. And, to me, this chapter is a beautiful shifting of priorities.

After reading his words, I can't help but ask myself:

What do I value?

What do I cherish?

What do I pursue?

Probably the most incredible part of our pursuit of wisdom is the fact that we will never "arrive." We always have room to grow in the wisdom department, and Solomon clearly acknowledges that. He doesn't say that he's got it all figured out or give a 10-step plan for living in perfect wisdom at all times. He doesn't even say that being the wisest person who ever lived is the goal of his writing.

Proverbs is a simple invitation to grow.

The acquisition of wisdom isn't instantaneous. It's not a destination at which we arrive but is a beautiful journey we have the privilege to walk out with the Lord. This is a daily practice and a muscle that develops over time.

If you're looking to gain all the wisdom in the world right at this moment, it's unlikely to happen. Sorry to break it to you. But the reason for the journey is a beautiful one: God cherishes being with us. A relationship with us, His children, is the thing He desires most in the world.

If we want wisdom, we need to be spending time with Him.

Have you ever spent so much time around someone that you began to pick up their mannerisms? There are certain phrases that I say now because friends of mine say them frequently. I have picked up some facial expressions because I've hung out regularly with certain people, or worse, binge-watched too much of a particular television show. The truth is, we tend to become like who we hang out with, including God.

So, this is your formal invitation to spend time with Him. Search the Scriptures, engage with His Word, meet with Him in prayer, worship Him with your heart, soul, mind, and strength, and seek out truth in the context of godly community. Spend some time in the quiet of nature, have coffee with an encouraging friend, and fill up journals by writing about the goodness of God. Because the more we search after Him and the more time we spend with Him, the more we'll become like Him.

Wisdom shouldn't be our ultimate goal, a relationship with God should be. And, because of that precious relationship with the One who created us all, wisdom will be a natural byproduct.

Reflection

Why do you want wisdom?

God given wisdom - There are millions of critical decisions we are faced with in our lives. Wisdom from God helps me in making decisions based on God's truth in the bible - his ways not my own or my fleshly desires.
Prov. 2:11 - Wise choices will watch over you.

How do you try to gain wisdom?

Prayer, listening to God, seeking out biblical resources, learning from others' experiences + advice.

What is God saying to you?

Give yourself grace and have patients.

DAY 3: PROVERBS 2

Read Proverbs Chapter 2.

What stood out to you in today's Proverb?

Cry out for insight & ask for understanding.

Search for them...seek them.

This = Fear of the Lord & the knowledge of God.

From His Mouth come knowledge & understanding

His words   The bible

Honesty
Integrity
Just
Faithfulness
Godly

I am a big fan of achievement. I want to be the best, and I want to accomplish many things. Historically, this has meant relationship and fun being placed on the back burner in favor of making progress on specific goals.

Achieving is where I've found my identity for the majority of my life. I've thought, very incorrectly, that to know who I am, provide any value to society, or be accepted by others, I need to perform.

Instead of focusing on becoming who God has called me to be, I've dedicated much of my time to accomplishing tasks and honing skills.

What Do You Spend Time Pursuing?

While reading this Proverb, I was struck by the author's urgency. He's begging the reader to pursue wisdom whole-heartedly. He knew the immense treasure that wisdom is and didn't want anyone to miss out on it! This gift isn't something that we should put off seeking out until tomorrow but is readily available for us today.

Typically, when I think of pursuit, I think of a prey and predator situation, but that's not at all the meaning. Wisdom doesn't elude us or run from us if we search after it, but longs to be found. When we seek God, we will find wisdom in copious amounts. We don't need to conquer, subdue, or strive to achieve wisdom because it isn't dependent upon us.

Wisdom isn't something that we manufacture or sustain ourselves. It's a precious gift that is freely given to us by a loving Father who wants nothing but the best for us. It's an invaluable treasure.

What Are You Valuing?

The truth is that we pursue the things we value: that position, that relationship, that goal, that trip. If we see something or someone as a priority, we will go out of our way to obtain the desired outcome.I don't know what you're currently valuing, but I can guarantee that you're pursuing those things or people in some way.

If our professed value-system and our actions don't match, that points to a problem. If we say that we value our jobs but we aren't willing to put forth a concerted effort, there's a mismatch. If we say we value family, but we aren't willing to talk to any of them during tough times, there could be a problem there. If we claim to value our relationship with God, but we never spend time with Him or His people, that could warrant some further examination.

Our pursuit always reveals our value system. Recently, I realized that I have valued and pursued self-protection for much of my life. While I do trust God, I'm beginning to see that I tend to trust myself more, which sounds silly when I type it out for all the world to read. The majority of my actions (especially my unhealthy ones) stem from the lie that I need to protect myself from the potential dangers around me. My pursuit of self-protection revealed my out of whack value system.

Having the Courage to About-Face

At the beginning of 2018, I felt a pull to steal away with God and spend some intentional time with Him. He wanted to heal certain parts of me that I didn't realize were broken. Though I protested for a while, I'm so thankful that I did obey in time. He revealed some hurts I had ignored and restored parts of my identity that had become defined by anyone and anything other than Him.

As I submitted to the process, I noticed that my pursuit changed as my values changed. When I no longer saw myself as a machine that was created for work and achievement, and instead saw myself as a daughter of God, achieving was no longer my ultimate pursuit. When I understood that God loves me and I don't need to protect myself from Him, self-protection no longer had to be my primary focus. Because my values changed, I could be free to pursue relationships, create with abandon, and dare to take risks I never would've dreamed of before. But it all started with my identity and my values.

Taking the time to assess our values and pursuit can unearth some interesting things we didn't know were there. While this is by no means an easy process, I encourage you to sit with God and think over these questions today.

Give God some space to stir your affections, highlight your value system, and reveal what you're currently pursuing. It's my hope and prayer that you can hear what He's saying, even when it hurts, knowing that He is the most important relationship for us to pursue. After all, closeness with Him is how we are created to live.

Reflection

Who or what do you pursue?

Outer beauty more than inner or
spiritual beauty

Family & friends

Praise & affirmation

Healing & wisdom

New skills/learning
Adventure

Who or what do your actions say you treasure?

Earthly things more than
heavenly treasure.

What is God saying to you? Give yourself Grace
Learn to become more self-discipline
Focus on becoming who God has
called me be?

God,
who have you called me to
be? What does that look
like? How do I accomplish
this?

Wisdom longs to be found

DAY 4: PROVERBS 3

Read Proverbs Chapter 3.

What stood out to you in today's Proverb?

Parents teach their children.

Wear loyalty + kindness like a necklace always reminding you of the character qualities within ourselves to exude to find favor with both God + people.

How do I trust with all my heart???

Trust in the Lord with all your heart, do not lean on your own understanding.

Seek His will in all you do and he will show you which path to take.

Proverbs 3:5-6 are probably some of the most famous verses in all the Bible. These life-giving words are printed on mugs, t-shirts, magnets, and bumper stickers. And, because these words are so visible, they're easy for me to neglect—they've lost some of the sweetness they once had. It's as if I think I have a license to gloss over them because I have these verses memorized. Sadly, I don't sit and dig into them like I once did.

I am confident that I'm not alone in this, so I want to take these verses line by line and see what God wants to say to us through them. Whether you've heard these a million times before or this is your first time, let's sit with them and see what we discover!

What Does it Mean to Trust?

Trust is an area in which I've struggled for many years because self-protection is one of my top priorities. Due to past hurts, I give myself out selectively and sparingly. I rarely depend on anyone other than myself and there are few people in whom I put my whole confidence.

I even allowed this habit to color my view of God. I've been disappointed by people, so it's easy for me to expect to be disappointed by God. I've lived through things like abuse and neglect, and for many years, I was sure that God would treat me the same way. I've been lied to, even by people who had beautiful intentions, so it can be difficult for me to trust the truthfulness of God. Thankfully He is patient with me as I'm slowly learning to believe Him. He doesn't stand around with arms crossed, tapping His foot at me with a scowl on his face. Instead, He calmly and kindly invites me closer, celebrating the small victories in my life.

The truth is that our hearts were created to trust God. We were made to be in lock-step with Him, following Him, not out of obligation but out of a loving and healthy relationship. We are limited, finite human beings who were made to depend on Him. He doesn't fail. He doesn't break our confidence. He doesn't abandon or betray us. He is worthy of our trust.

What Does "With All Your Heart" Mean to You?

I'm great at compartmentalization. Work is in one compartment, friends in another, family in another, and church in another. God has His box—one that is beautiful, tidy, and breathtaking. And emotions are shoved in a dimly-lit corner, so they don't mess up the well-organized and maintained box collection I have created.

For years, I thought I was the only one who did this, until I began sharing my life and story with others who had done the same thing. This unhealthy heart option helps us navigate our 21st-century lives so, even if it doesn't serve us well all the time, we stick with it. But God doesn't long for just one section of our lives or hearts—He wants it all.

He doesn't want us to look good on the outside while withering within. He wants a deep and all-encompassing relationship with each of us. He wants us to know that we're His children and we are fully loved. Our hearts can have many different loves, but, chiefly, we were made to love and be loved by God. Once we're confident of this truth, we can courageously love Him freely, putting the other loves of our hearts in their rightful places. *show me how*

I encourage you, as we venture through the entire book of Proverbs, to regularly check in with your heart. Take a moment each day to examine if you love comfort more than Him, if you're trusting yourself more than relying on Him, or if you've put your emotions on the shelf instead of allowing yourself to feel as you were created to feel.

Trusting God with all of our hearts, not just specific compartments, is how we were made to live. And I believe every day is an invitation from God to do just that. If we've done a poor job of loving God with all our hearts in the recent past, that's okay, today's a brand new start and a fresh invitation to trust Him more deeply. This is a life-long learning experience and one that God is pleased to walk with us.

To be Continued...

These verses contain so much within them that I don't want to rush through them. We're going to sit here for one more day and listen to what the Lord has to say about our hearts, our minds, and our ways. So, tomorrow we will pick up right where we've left off and finish this particular Proverb.

Reflection

Who or what do you trust? Why?

Trust - firm belief in the reliability, truth, ability or strength of someone or something.
I trust God + that he loves me unconditionally.
I trust in my mom that she will always be there for me to help me with a task if I ask her for help.
I trust Credence + Calah
I trust the bible to be true.
I trust my job to always be there
B/c of being let down + hurt, I have a hard time trusting.

Are there any parts or compartments of your heart that you aren't yet entrusting to God? Why do you think that is?

God,
It really is a terrible feeling to realize I have such a hard time trusting...due to hurt, pain, dissappointments, let downs, lack of relationship.
It's not that I want an instant fix - I know it takes time, God... I've given it time - lots of time work energy - I'm exhausted + at the end of my rope. I feel like I have nothing else, I don't want to give up, but I am tired. I'm sad.
I'm restless. I'm down. I'm broken, I'm empty
I'm numb w/out feeling.

What is God saying to you?

I don't know... God please open my ears to hear + my heart to recieve. and my mind to understand.

DAY 5: PROVERBS 3

Read Proverbs Chapter 3.

What stood out to you in today's Proverb?

God show me, teach me how to
trust in you with all my heart

I can't lean on my own
understanding... b/c it is NOTHING!
↓ my understanding   anyway
↘ confusing
leads to pain
non existent
wrong

My impatience is making me mad
& frustrated.

Why?.

Joyful is the person who
finds wisdom = the
one who gains
understanding.

As promised, we're going to finish out Proverbs 3:5-6. I pray these verses go beyond some phrases that we've simply memorized over the years to applicable truths that change how we live.

Avoiding Leaning on Your Own Understanding

A few years ago, I fell and chipped the bone in my ankle, an experience that forced me to depend on others. It happened over an hour away from home, and we weren't going back for another few days, so I sat with my foot iced and elevated, praying that it would miraculously heal itself so I could go back to being wholly dependent upon myself again. Now, looking back, I'm thankful that I wasn't miraculously healed because I had a valuable lesson to learn.

One night, a bonfire was scheduled, complete with songs, s'mores, and loads of fun. But there was a problem: I couldn't walk out there. I couldn't put weight on my right foot and there was no way I would be able to hop on one foot all the way out to the bonfire. I pridefully wanted to figure it out myself without relying on anyone else, but that wasn't in the cards. Instead, two friends gave me their shoulders and let me lean on them when I couldn't make it on my own.

As I've been thinking about this idea of leaning not on my own understanding, I keep going back to these sweet friends of mine who were willing to take my weight when I couldn't carry myself. Though I wanted to do it all on my own, they wouldn't let me be stubborn. They wore me down and protected me from myself at that moment. Had I not leaned on them, insisting instead on my way, I would have likely ended up causing more damage to myself.

This verse isn't saying that we shouldn't be intelligent or that we shouldn't use wisdom. It's just a reminder that God has a better plan. He sees the full picture, He knows all the variables, and He knows exactly what's coming our way.

The Bible talks about us only being able to see in part, which means that we don't have all of the information when making decisions. There have been so many times when God has changed my course even though I thought I had a perfect plan laid out. Each time I've wondered why He has me doing something I feel is so illogical but, in the end, I've found that His ways are indeed better than mine (Isaiah 55:8-9).

How Can You Acknowledge Him in All Your Ways?

The word "acknowledge" could also be translated as know, perceive, consider, or declare. But the translation that strikes me the most is "acquaintance." Because God is so deeply relational, it only makes sense for a relational word, such as this, to be used in this context.

The truth is that God wants to know all your ways! He doesn't long for this information because He's nosy or wants to learn something bad so He can punish you. He wants to be acquainted with all your ways of thinking, feeling, and doing because He loves you deeply.

Have you invited God into those spaces?
Have you taken the time to introduce Him to your ways?
Have you asked His opinion?
Have you asked His advice?

This doesn't always have to be a long, drawn-out process (though there are times when that is necessary), but tends to happen in the mundane, day-to-day moments of life. It's like stopping to pray in the moment instead of just *saying* you'll pray about a decision. Or setting aside that intentional quiet time every day to get more acquainted with the One who loves you. Or sharing the good, the bad, and the ugly about how you're doing with Him.

Introducing Him to all of our ways can feel awkward at first, but for me, the fact that He already knows every thought, feeling, intention, and action takes a little pressure off.

Do You Believe He'll Make Your Paths Straight?

There's so much beauty in the Hebrew word *yashar* from which we get the phrase "direct" or "make straight." It means to make the affairs of the person prosper. So, if we're acknowledging Him, calling Him Lord, and submitting our entire lives to Him, then our paths are going to be pleasant. Not because of any external or tertiary benefits — but because of Him.

The truth is this: God is the ultimate prize. More than any other earthly benefit we can receive — more than money in the bank, food on the table, and other forms of pleasantness — God is our treasure. And, as we spend more time with Him, we'll begin to experience this more and more. We don't spend time with Him to try to manipulate Him into giving us something good. We don't have to feel insecure or worry if He'll come through because the Bible says He gives good gifts to His children (James 1:17) and He fulfilled our greatest need (Romans 8:32) while we were still His enemies (Romans 5:10). He is a good and loving God who loves spending time with you! Let's choose to sit in His presence today!

God,
Show me any areas in which I am
not submitting my entire life to you.
I want to grow and in that is being
aware of things that I may be
unaware of. Open my eyes to see.

Reflection

What areas are you leaning on your own understanding? How can you lean upon God instead?

The truth is... I don't even trust my own understanding enough to lean on it. I question my understanding more than anything.

the problem is I'm not fully trusting God either. I seem to stay in a state of uncertainty + worry. I don't give myself grace like God would want me to. I have been impatient + get down because I take steps back when all I want is to move forward

Is God acquainted with your ways? Are there any parts of your life you don't want to introduce to God?

I feel like I am open with God about my struggles, my confusion + uncertainty. This is what it is like to have a constant thorn in my side. Annoying I lay it all at your feet God. I have nothing left in me. I avoid by distractions - phone, business, dating

What is God saying to you?

Reread the sermon I wrote
for seminary.

DAY 6: PROVERBS 4

Read Proverbs Chapter 4.

What stood out to you in today's Proverb?

Listen, Seek, search, find

Verse 20-23
Pay attention to what I say
Listen to my words
Distractions ← Don't lose sight of them
Lies
Let them penetrate deep into
your heart (MEDITATE)

For they (His words) bring life
to those who FIND them &
healing to their whole body
— physical, mental

Seek, search, listen, meditate,
find, keep

Renewing of our minds

When I read through Proverbs 4 while preparing to write this devotional, verses 23-27 stood out to me like a flashing neon sign. They caught my attention and captivated me. I knew there was a depth to these verses that I hadn't mined before and I was excited to spend time digging into each verse individually.

We're going to do the same thing and spend the next few days taking each verse line by line. It's going to be tempting to fly through or skip over these verses, but I'm going to ask you to resist that urge. I believe these verses are foundational for the rest of the book and integral for us to live healthily and wisely.

One of the things that stood out to me the most about Proverbs 4:23-27 is the order of the instructions. We are told to take care of our hearts first because the heart influences the rest of the list: speech, focus, the mind, and our actions. I believe each of these areas builds upon the one that immediately precedes it. I have found that if I'm struggling with an issue in one of the areas mentioned in these verses, I can always return to the state of my heart and identify a potential source of the problem.

I wouldn't have been willing to discuss the heart like this a year ago because I thought my heart was untrustworthy. I thought it was terrible, damaged, and destined to remain that way. I thought that because I'm more of a thinker than a feeler, verses like this about the heart didn't apply to me. I zeroed in on instructions about the mind or our strength because I was more comfortable with those. But the heart was off limits (or so I thought).

Let's Carefully Examine Our Hearts

In May 2018, I took a week-long sabbatical, which was an unusual occurrence in my world because, as a general rule, I don't take time off. I work and work and then work some more. I've gotten better over the years about making time for people and fitting some downtime into my schedule, but I've never not worked for an entire week. And that's exactly what I did.

During this week off I kept hearing God say, "I want your heart."

But I protested. "God, you don't want my heart. It's ugly. It's gross. It's not worth your time. It's dry, hard, and cracked. I've neglected it, leaving it out in the elements to fend for itself. I've ignored its cries for help. Trust me, God, you don't want this thing."

"I want your heart."

"I'll give you my mind. Or my strength. Or my skills. But you don't want my heart."

"I want your heart."

What I hadn't realized is precisely what this verse in Proverbs says: everything flows from the heart. If my heart is entirely devoted to Him, it will saturate everything else I do, say, or think. When I have His life pumping through my veins and into every single part of my body, I don't need to worry about what the rest of my actions will be like because He will motivate them.

Learning to Inform the Heart

For years, I was preoccupied with my actions, focused on how they would look or affect others. I thought I could control myself enough so that I would be okay. I just had to be kind enough, helpful enough, or smart enough. I had to resort to a behavior modification plan because I wasn't on board with God's heart replacement plan.

But when we care for and guard our hearts, we begin to see life-change. I'm freer now than I've ever been before. I'm more empathetic than I've ever been before. I'm more trusting than I've ever been before. I already see such a difference within myself, and I'm still very new on this journey.

There's still a lot for me to learn on the subject of guarding my heart, but I'm so thankful to be walking this out. Instead of condemning, ignoring, or giving in to every impulse of the heart, let's inform our hearts with God's truth and guard it with all vigilance. — Meditation   — what does God's word say?

Let's put God's Word to the test and see what happens!

Reflection

What's the state of your heart?

The state of my heart... well I could sugar coat it and say my heart is happy, full, kind, giving + pure and this is all true, but I am cognizant of the fact that my heart is not all good. It can be selfish, self seeking, sinful. It can, at times, be hardened + blind.

Do you believe that God wants your heart? Why or why not?

yes, because of his transformative power.

because He wants relationship with us,

so he can cherish it, renew it, speak life to you

What is God saying to you?

I care what you think of me, God.

DAY 7: PROVERBS 4

Read Proverbs Chapter 4.

What stood out to you in today's Proverb?

Listen. Pay attention. Learn
His guidance is good.

Seek to find wisdom. - Exactly why
you started this book.

Yesterday, we dove into Proverbs 4:23 and focused on the heart—the wellspring of life. God wants our hearts because He knows that everything we think, do, or say flows from it. Today, we're going to build upon that foundation by focusing on the next verse, Proverbs 4:24, which is all about our speech. The truth is, as we guard our hearts, knowing the life contained therein, our speech will change as a natural byproduct.

What does it mean to put away deceitful speech, like the author instructs?
What would it look like to put away all fraudulent claims?

Though I'm sure none of us would like to admit it, we all tell lies from time to time. There are the "little white lies" that we think don't matter that much. And there are the bigger lies we tell that are incredibly damaging, lies we hope and pray no one will ever find out. We even tell lies to ourselves. And I think that's where we need to begin.

What lies do you tell yourself (and others) to make yourself seem better than you actually are?
Do you ever lie to make yourself sound less than you actually are?

I've walked this line for years! In certain settings, I would talk myself up and inflate my resume. Anytime anyone would begin talking about their accomplishments I would try to find a way to top them. I would make sure I had an answer for every question because the phrase "I don't know" was unacceptable in my vocabulary. I had to be right, I had to be the best, and I had to top everyone else—even if that meant stretching the truth.

Simultaneously, I would berate myself. I would talk down to myself. I didn't like me, and I made sure I knew it. My self-talk was not life-giving and it was deeply harmful. This form of self-deprecation fed my need to exaggerate in front of others which fed into the unhealthy cycle.

I'm sure I'm not alone.

We all have this impulse to put on a front so we'll be liked—it just looks a little different from person to person. Maybe you have to know all the answers or have a solution to every problem. Perhaps you always have to contribute something to the conversation— you have to fill the silence with many words because, well, that's what you do. Or maybe you like to put up a facade that you think others will like more than the reality of who you are. Or perhaps you habitually inflate your resume.

While the way we do it might vary from person to person or situation to situation, most of us exaggerate our accomplishments, our skills, our exploits, or ourselves.

The other side of the coin is when we are filled with self-deprecation. Maybe you put yourself down and doubt your skills. Perhaps you tell yourself that you're not good enough and shrink away because the self-talk you've engaged in has hurt you. Or maybe you're repeating the lies you've been told all your life.

While the way we do it might change from person to person or situation to situation, most of us exaggerate our failures, our mistakes, and our sins, forgetting the goodness of the One who has saved us.

But what if we put those things away?

What if we just choose to be ourselves?

My speech, both the exaggerations of my skills and the magnifications of my failures, revealed my belief: I thought I was worthless. Because I felt I was the worst, I would berate myself. Because I believed I didn't have worth, I would try to earn worth through the things I did. I didn't know I could be worthy any other way.

But, in order to fix my speech problem, I need to fix my heart problem. It's not a matter of simply removing some words from my vocabulary. It's about taking what God says about me and accepting that as truth. This is a continual process for me.

Changing my speech isn't something that has happened instantaneously. It's a continual growth opportunity. There are fleeting thoughts that run through my mind, lies that I have to stop and replace with truth. I have to remind myself of the goodness of God. I have to tell myself that I'm a child who He wholeheartedly loves and is entirely pleased with. I have to remind my heart that it's safe.

Today, I encourage you to look at what your speech reveals about how you see you. Then allow God to heal those parts of you. Let truth replace and drown out the lies you've come to believe. And, as God begins to heal those places, I believe your speech will start to change. I know that's been the case for me.

Reflection

What do you say about yourself? To yourself?

There are times I'm not kind to myself or I don't give myself grace. I have become better at stopping in my tracks and replacing lies/negative thinking with truth + uplifting encouragement.

What do these things reveal about the state of your heart?

The state of my heart is wobble - somewhat like a teeter totter at times. It takes a real conscious effort sometimes to use my brain + knowledge of God's truth about me.

What is God saying to you?

Have patience in the process- Years
of not thinking positive about myself
won't just change overnight. It takes
prayer, willingness to change +
work on my part.

DAY 8: PROVERBS 4

Read Proverbs Chapter 4.

What stood out to you in today's Proverb?

We've already discussed the importance of our hearts and how we are to care for them diligently. Yesterday, we focused on putting deceitful speech behind us, especially the exaggerations we make about ourselves, to ourselves and others. Our speech is a barometer for the state of our hearts that we have the privilege of monitoring. Today, we're going to move on to Proverbs 4:25 and turn our focus to our *focus*.

We Are Responsible For Guarding Our Gaze

This is more than just an arbitrary form of censorship. It's meant to be a meaningful look at our focus. If we're focusing on our own pleasure, then we might be more inclined to look at things we know aren't good for our long-term well-being. If we're focusing on getting ahead in life, we might be tempted to look at people as commodities instead of human beings. If we're focusing on pleasing other people, we might begin to lose ourselves. And if we're not focusing on God, then we'll miss out on the richness He has for us.

So let's dig deep and take a good look at where our focus lies.

I'm a pretty focused person. When I know what I'm working toward and where I'm going, I will generally find a way to get there. When I want to, I can tune out distractions so I can focus on what's important, whether a project or a person. So it only makes sense for this to be one of my favorite verses!

I love the determination of focus, but I hate how distracted I can become in the things that truly matter.

While I am great at maintaining my focus in some areas, I'm distracted by comfort, entertainment, achievement, and more. I'm distracted by myself and all I want to accomplish. I'm distracted by the things I've left undone. I'm distracted by those who are doing the things I want to be doing. I'm distracted by my overwhelming desire to be right and be in control.

What Are You Distracted By?

This verse reminds me of the story found in Matthew 14 where Peter walked on water. The disciples were in their boat together, having a terrible time as they struggled to make their way across the sea to their next location. But then they saw something that freaked them out: Jesus walking on water. They thought it was a ghost, until Jesus spoke. Then Peter pulled a "Peter" and told Jesus to call him out on the water. And Jesus did.

Then, Peter walked on water. *Are you kidding me?* Keep in mind, this didn't happen on an evening with optimal water-walking conditions. The winds were strong, and the disciples had been fighting them all night. The waves were probably crashing, and the sea was likely rough. And it's in these conditions that Peter asked Jesus to call him out, a call that he answered.

Can you imagine how crazy this experience must have been for him? I would've been looking all over the place! I would've looked down at my feet and then back at the disciples to rub in the fact that they didn't think of the idea first. I would have looked up at the ominous sky, at the roaring waves, and in my excitement, I likely would've been looking at everyone *except* for Jesus. In the story, when Peter took his eyes off of Jesus, he became afraid and began to sink.

Have you ever experienced the fear that comes when we take our eyes off Jesus? I know I have! It's amazing how quickly I can go from faith to fear when my focus gets derailed. I have found that when I take a leap of faith in obedience to God, I'm not worried or fearful as long as I'm paying attention to Him. When I get distracted or begin focusing on the facts of my situation, anxiety starts to overwhelm me. I can quickly become paralyzed, just like Peter did, when my focus shifts and I become distracted.

Distraction, just like our speech, can reveal our heart posture. If I'm always being pulled away by things that are far inferior to

God and His goodness, then it reveals a problem with the things I love. When my focus strays from God, it's a sweet reminder that my "loves" are out of whack and I need to return to Him.

It's my hope and prayer that each of us would be willing to stop and take a look at how we use our time, where our money goes, and what we set our gaze upon to identify where our focus is. Then, if there's anything out of place with our focus, I pray we will dare to make the necessary adjustments to our hearts. I hope we will care for our hearts and stir up our affections for Him as we go about our days.

A PROVERB A DAY

Reflection

Where is your focus? Do you find yourself getting distracted often?

What does your focus say about the state of your heart?

46

What is God saying to you?

DAY 9: PROVERBS 4

Read Proverbs Chapter 4.

What stood out to you in today's Proverb?

This week, we've covered so much ground within this one chapter, and we're not done yet! Upon the backdrop of guarding our focus, speaking truthfully, and treasuring our hearts, we will launch into a discussion about our mind and our thoughts.

I've always been drawn to this verse because I pride myself on my ability to ponder. For years, I valued my mind more than any other part of me because I believe it's my greatest asset. This is fine and dandy until my pride gets involved. Then I go from praising God for how he made me to praising myself because I think I'm so great. I can easily fall into the trap of thinking I know all the answers and that I'm always right, instead of continually relying upon God. I can make the mistake of doing what I *think* is right instead of what is *actually* right.

Your Formal Invitation to Think About Thinking

The word "ponder" found in Proverbs 4:26 can also be translated "make level." The word is indicative of rolling a cylinder over something again and again until it becomes flat. And that's what we're called to do. We're supposed to make level our paths, going over them again and again with the truth, until we're able to walk securely. And that process begins with the mind.

The truth is, we all have rocky patches in our thinking. These are the thoughts that trip you up, the memories that put you in an unhealthy downward thought spiral, or the lies you believe about yourself—even when presented with the contrary. Certain thought patterns are familiar, worn, and leave me beaten up and bruised every time.

I think what I'm doing isn't as good as what others are doing.

I doubt the impact my words can make on those around me.

I obsess over the mistakes I've made, especially the little ones.

I forget I've already forgiven people who have hurt me.

And it's not just the large ruts that can cause us trouble. The right pebble at the right spot on the path can send us into a toxic thought tailspin.

The one poorly-worded message.

The off-handed comment from the boss.

The person's post on social media.

The bit of unexpected news.

Smoothing Out Thought Processes With the Word

Here's the truth: no one is exempt from this. We all have parts of our minds that are a bit rocky and need to be smoothed out. Thankfully, we don't have to figure this out on our own. In Romans 12, Paul tells us to renew our minds so that we can know God's will because, at the end of the day, that's the most important thing we can know. He reminds us that consistent submission to Christ is essential to the life of a person who is following God. Smoothing the uneven paths in our minds is not a result of brute force or sheer willpower—it comes from steeping our minds in the Word of God.

Just like the rest of the verses we've covered, it all comes back to the heart. Our minds are directly related to our hearts. If we have thought problems, rocky thinking, or unhealthy self-talk—at the end of the day, what we really have is a heart problem.

For years, I thought I just needed to fill my mind with facts about God and then it would be renewed. If I knew all about God, then the knowing should be enough to change my life. As a result, I could spout off facts about the Bible but still remain hard as a stone during moments of worship or prayer. I went through the motions of loving God, but I didn't honestly feel affection toward Him. I couldn't change my heart via my mind, but I can change my mind by changing my heart.

If you find yourself with some rocky thought patterns, I encourage you to look at how or if you're renewing your mind. The thought patterns that trip us up reveal a great deal about our hearts and where our affections lie.

Reflection

Do you have any rocky patches in your mind?

What do your thoughts say about the state of your heart?

What is God saying to you?

DAY 10: PROVERBS 4

Read Proverbs Chapter 4.

What stood out to you in today's Proverb?

Today, we will discuss the last verse in Proverbs 4, building upon the foundation we've laid this week. These verses remind us that God isn't so much about behavior modification as He is about heart transformation. Because our hearts inform our speech, where our focus lies, and the way we think—we are to educate our hearts with truth and turn our affections toward God. As we do this, our actions will begin to change.

One of the questions I'm beginning to ask myself with some frequency is this: "What do my actions show that I believe?" This is not a fun question to answer honestly.

Habits Reveal the State of the Heart

When I'm elbow-deep into a bag of junk food I shouldn't be eating, I could say that I just love to eat. But the reality might actually be that I don't feel well and I'm seeking comfort in food.

When I'm on hour six of binge-watching my favorite show with no plans on leaving the house or talking to another human, I could say that I'm just doing some self-care. But the reality might be that I'm isolating because I am scared to be known and terrified of rejection.

When I'm up working until 4 a.m., I could say that I'm passionate about and dedicated to my work. But the reality might be that I see my body as a commodity created to work instead of something to be cared for.

These are three tendencies I fall into with some regularity that reveal my desire for comfort above all else—above stewarding my body well, pursuing relationships, and, at times, even seeking Him. My feet will long to go on the path of least resistance, one that will bring me the most comfort possible—but that's not where God calls me to go.

Our actions sure do reveal a lot about the posture of our hearts when we take the time to examine them. What do your actions reveal about what or who you love?

Bearing Fruit is a Slow Process

As we learn to inform our hearts, remove deceitful speech from our vocabularies, focus on what Christ has done for us, and level out the rocky parts of our minds, our behaviors will begin to change. As we intentionally fill our minds and hearts with God's Word, our loves will become aligned with the things of God and harmful behaviors won't have the same pull they used to. The Bible tells us that it's sharper than any sword and can cut through our layers of hurt, pain, and falsities. It also has this transformative power, where bad is replaced by good, and we are restored and refreshed.

Sometimes the changes are apparent right away, and other times, they're much more subtle. I didn't have this big, obvious, outward sin problem, but I was dealing with death and lies in my mind and heart. As the Lord has been healing and restoring those parts of me, I've become more open, more honest, more transparent, and more free. And lately, people have been mentioning it. I've been in this process for over six months, and the fruit is starting to come to the surface.

I encourage you to consider your actions, examine what they reveal about your heart, and then put in the hard work necessary to transform those parts of your heart that aren't in line with His Word. The great part of this is that we're not responsible for changing our behavior on our own. Our change is a natural result of becoming more like God. As you examine yourself, ask for His help, His opinion, and His guidance. He is the one who changes, heals, and restores us. We only have to be willing.

Let's invite Him to transform us and let's start today!

Reflection

What do your actions say about the state of your heart?

Do you ever grow impatient with the transformation process?

What is God saying to you?

DAY 11: PROVERBS 5

Read Proverbs Chapter 5.

What stood out to you in today's Proverb?

Adultery is one of those topics that no one wants to talk about—ever. But did you know that adultery is a common theme throughout the Bible? It's found in the Law of the Old Testament, the books written by the prophets, the letters written by the apostles, and was even mentioned by Jesus. Since adultery is a hot topic for God, we're going to discuss it, even if it makes some of us (including me) feel uncomfortable.

If you're single and you've never been married, or you're divorced even though you did nothing wrong, you might be thinking to yourself, *I haven't committed adultery. I don't have to pay attention to this one.* If that's you, I get it. I'm in the same boat. I'm single, so I've always breezed over the verses and chapters about adultery, making a mental note to check them out later when they're more applicable.

But the truth is that they're applicable today because I'm in a deep and committed relationship with Christ. More so, these verses are a warning to me because I'm prone to wander from Him. My natural tendency is to be an adulterer at heart. That's an awkward sentence to write but is an incredibly accurate description of my state.

Developing an Infidelity Habit

Sin is tempting and can be fun in the moment. It sounds like a great idea at the time, but it always leads to death. Gossiping about someone might make me feel good in the moment but it leads to relational problems and mistrust. Lying seems like a brilliant idea to get out of a situation but doing so only hurts my credibility and is not in line with the heart and character of God. Yelling at someone is a great way to let off steam, but the guilt that bubbles up afterward is gnawing.

Even with this knowledge, I still find myself, over and over again, doing things I know are wrong or straying from the things I know to be true and right. The truth is that each time I do so, I am the adulterer this chapter warns about.

Because I know my internal battle with sin and just how often I wander away from God, I struggle to accept that He loves me. I honestly can't believe that He would choose me! I am the adulterer who runs away from the One who loves me, and still, He picked me to be His bride. More than that, He continues choosing me no matter how many times I stray. Our God truly is amazing!

Learning that We are Greatly Loved

Fidelity, intimacy, and commitment are words that send shivers down my spine. These concepts are so foreign to me that I'm not entirely sure how to live them out. But God is patient and kind toward me. Even when I mess up, even when I sin against Him, even when I'm adulterous, He still accepts and forgives me. He doesn't turn His back on me, but instead kindly invites me back to Him.

This Proverb reminds me of the story in Luke 7 where the sinful woman crashes a Pharisee's dinner party. Jesus was at a Pharisee's house sitting down to eat when a woman with a bad reputation showed up. But she didn't bat an eye. She washed Jesus's feet with her tears, wiped them with her hair, and then anointed Jesus with oil. The religious guys stared at her, shocked by her actions and Jesus's allowance of this behavior. And then Jesus shared something so profound: our love is in direct correlation to how much we've been forgiven. This woman had been forgiven of so much that she loved Jesus extravagantly. But if we think we don't need to be forgiven or that our sins are "no big deal" then our capacity to love will decrease.

This Proverb reminds me that I am that woman. I am just as guilty as she was and just as forgiven as she was. Her response to the love of Jesus is the perfect example of how I should respond to Him. This chapter helps me understand the reality that I am not the one who has been forgiven little, but I am the one who has been forgiven much.

I encourage you to sit with God today and let His love wash over you. My hope and prayer is that we would accept what He's done for us and be confident in how He feels for us. And that we would bubble over with love and praise, knowing we are significantly loved and forgiven of much.

Reflection

Do you love God greatly? Do you believe He loves you greatly?

Are you an adulterer at heart? Use this time to pray and repent.

What is God saying to you?

DAY 12: PROVERBS 6

Read Proverbs Chapter 6.

What stood out to you in today's Proverb?

.

There's so much in this Proverb that we can talk about. The carelessness of our words, the things God hates, and keeping distance from adulterers are a few of the highlights. But as I was writing this chapter, none of these topics felt right to discuss. I started and restarted this particular day, over and over again, taking a different route with this chapter each time — but it wasn't until I reread the passage, for what felt like the hundredth time, that it finally hit me.

"My son, keep your father's commandment,

and forsake not your mother's teaching.

Bind them on your heart always;

tie them around your neck.

When you walk, they will lead you;

when you lie down, they will watch over you;

and when you awake, they will talk with you.

For the commandment is a lamp and the teaching a light,

and the reproofs of discipline are the way of life..."

Proverbs 6:20-23

These verses, in no uncertain terms, instruct the reader to listen to Solomon's commandments and follow his instruction. These will keep us out of trouble and our feet on the right path. He says that the commandments of wisdom and teachings from God are a lamp unto our feet. (Sounds a little bit like some verses in Psalms, doesn't it?)

What struck me about these verses is that something will always be guiding us, we just have to decide what that is.

What Are You Binding Around Your Neck?

Whether we like to admit it or not, we pick up things from our environments. I am, by nature, a workaholic entrepreneur who represses her feelings and avoids pain because those are the things I was taught from an early age. I've battled, and am battling, various addictions and mental health struggles — partially because of my genes and partly because these things were normalized for me. In many ways, I'm a product of my past.

But those aren't the things I need to wear around my neck. They're not what I should listen to when deciding the way my feet should take me. However, they are my default setting.

Without the cross, I would have no hope of walking in a way worthy of being called a daughter of God. Without Jesus's perfect sacrifice on my behalf, I wouldn't have the ability to love and serve others. Without the eternal, unfailing love of God, I would happily live in my sinful nature, sure that it was the best way to cope with the hardships of life.

Following God's commandments daily is something I think we all have room to grow in. Am I perfect at this? By no means! Nor do I think I will ever be. But I have noticed, that day by day, as I seek Him, I want to follow His lead a little more than I did the day before.

I'm able to take off the belief that I need to earn love and accept that I am fully loved.

I can remove the lies of addiction and put on the new creation I am in Christ.

The workaholism badge I used to wear with such honor can be traded for rest and peace.

We all have something bound around our necks — words, actions, patterns, desires, lies, and truth — that we keep close to our hearts.

It's up to us to choose what those are. Every day we can decide whether we're going to listen to lies or listen to the truth. My hope and prayer for all of us is that today, we all remove something unhealthy from our necks, take a step forward, and allow the truth to illuminate our paths.

Reflection

What do you tend to bind around your neck? What do you keep close to your heart?

How does your life change when you bind God's Word around your neck?

What is God saying to you?

DAY 13: PROVERBS 7

Read Proverbs Chapter 7.

What stood out to you in today's Proverb?

When I read the Bible, I like to imagine what each person in the story is thinking, feeling, doing, or experiencing. I'll read it through once, taking in the story as a whole, but then I'll go back to the beginning and reread it from the perspective of a particular character. Then another character. Sometimes an on-looker or bystander. I repeat this process until I've gone through each character in the story.

I encourage you to try this with your favorite Bible story and see what you can learn about who God is, who you are, and how He feels about you.

When I focused on each of the characters in this Proverb, I saw this consistent theme: no matter our age, we can still fall prey to foolishness if we're not vigilant.

Let's dive in and see what we discover!

The Young Man

The man in this story is young, immature, and lacks wisdom. We've all been there. If you don't think so, I would encourage you to ask your parents or friends from your teenage years—I'm sure they'd be happy to refresh your memory.

I would dare to say there are areas of our lives where we *still* lack wisdom, no matter our age (I know that's the case for me). Though I'm much wiser than I once was, I still have a lot of room to grow in the area of wisdom. While we might be smart enough not to launch firecrackers in illegal areas, we might lack financial intelligence. Or we might be very savvy when it comes to business but lack wisdom when interacting with people.

The young man in our story wasn't vigilant and allowed himself to fall into temptation because he was wandering about in a part of town he shouldn't have been in, much later than he should've been out. He put himself in an undesirable position and opened himself up to the possibility of temptation.

This reminds me of the story of Adam and Eve. God told them they weren't to eat from a particular tree, but they ended up being tempted and eventually gave in. Have you ever thought about why the two of them were hanging around the tree they weren't allowed to eat from? The garden was probably vast and filled with lush plants to eat from and care for, and yet, they hung around the one tree with inedible fruit. They weren't using wisdom and set themselves up for failure, much like the young man we're reading about today.

While we might not be out and about actively looking to commit adultery or staking out a forbidden fruit tree, we can be tempted in little and big ways. But we're not alone in our temptation. The Bible tells us that the Holy Spirit is with us and helps us in our weakness. With His help, we can remain vigilant and courageously flee temptation when we encounter it.

The Woman

When I read through this Proverb again, I couldn't help but fixate on how this woman saw herself. I couldn't get past the fact that she didn't see herself the way God saw her. She didn't see herself and her body as precious and didn't value the covenant of marriage she had entered into. She foolishly pursued, enticed, and manipulated this man to sleep with her while her husband was away.

She was clearly in the wrong in this story, but I wholeheartedly believe that her incorrect behavior was rooted in a false view of herself.

It's so easy to fall into unhealthy behaviors when we believe lies about ourselves. *I'm not good enough. I'm too far gone. I'm a failure. I'm unlovable.* Each of these lies becomes an action: overachieving, outright rebellion, isolation, promiscuity, and more. If we believe lies as truth, then there's no reason to treat ourselves—our bodies, our gifts, our skills, our hearts, our minds—with respect, love, and care.

This woman's value system was out of whack, her priorities were in the wrong order, and she wasn't using wisdom. She hadn't heeded Solomon's advice and ended up hurting herself and others in the process.

The Woman's Husband

The woman's husband foolishly neglected his wife. He was gone often and wasn't set to return for some time. I wonder what he was doing so far away from home with a big bag of cash. The text doesn't say this, but I would imagine that he was probably running from something or avoiding someone. In the pursuit of his comfort or his ambition or both, he had neglected his wife and their home. Though she was responsible for committing adultery, he also played a part.

It's so easy to neglect things around us, especially if they're hard things. We want to overlook mending the relationship, neglect eating correctly or exercising regularly, and neglect taking the leap of faith to go after our dreams. We can neglect getting involved in our local church, meeting someone new, or cleaning our house or car. We can even ignore coming to God because He might call us out of our comfort zones. Though some are much more obvious than others, each instance of neglect can have far-reaching ramifications.

Overcoming Foolishness

This is a hard chapter to discuss, but I'm so glad we're walking through this together. Even though it's uncomfortable, increasing in wisdom starts with a realization of our lack. Then, with that knowledge in hand, we can come humbly to God, present those things to Him, and ask for forgiveness in our areas of need. We have the immense privilege of being loved and welcomed by the One with infinite wisdom at His disposal!

Each day is an opportunity to grow in wisdom, no matter how foolish we've been in the past. God is consistently giving us opportunities to humble ourselves, make changes, and gain more wisdom. Because we trust God with all of our hearts—leaning not on our own understanding, but trusting Him to make our paths straight—we don't have to end up like the characters in today's story.

I'm so incredibly grateful that we have the opportunity to choose a better way and pursue wisdom instead of folly.

Reflection

Do you relate to any of the characters in today's story? If so, how?

Are there any unhealthy behaviors you feel God is bringing to your attention? If so, what are the lies at the root of the behavior?

What is God saying to you?

DAY 14: PROVERBS 8

Read Proverbs Chapter 8.

What stood out to you in today's Proverb?

I'm not the blind-date type. I know some are, but for me—I feel it would be an incredibly awkward experience. The few times that my friends have even hinted at having someone they wanted to set me up with, their descriptions were severely lacking.

"He's 6'7" and an engineer."

"He's hilarious."

"He's just a nice guy."

That's about the extent of the information I've received from my friends about some of the guys they thought would be "perfect" for me. And, to each of these, I've responded with a hearty "no thanks."

But this leads me to wonder how my friends would describe me to someone if they were going to try and set me up with them.

A quirky workaholic?

A writer who never sleeps?

A devoted follower of Christ?

The world may never know...

What is Wisdom Like?

As I read through Proverbs 8, I found myself asking how I would describe wisdom based solely on this chapter. Or, if I were to try and set wisdom up on a blind date (a ridiculous visual, I know), how would I describe her? The writer gives us some excellent clues as to the character of wisdom in this particular chapter.

I encourage you to go through and see what character traits jump out to you. Here's what I spotted:

Noble

Inviting

Truthful

Righteous

Knowledgeable

Humble

Insightful

Available

Just

This list I've assembled can also be used to describe Jesus. Throughout the Gospels we see Jesus honoring others, inviting them into a relationship, and showering them with truth. He is perfectly righteous, entirely in the know, and the image of humility. Jesus sees into the heart, is always available, and just in every single word and action. He's all of these things and so much more! He is the one who is calling us and beckoning us to be wise — He's continually inviting us to be like Him.

Looking More Like Wisdom

Reading through the list, I can't help but ask myself how I measure up in comparison. Am I noble and inviting? Do I speak the language of truth, righteousness, and knowledge? Is my speech a sweet mixture of insight and humility? Do I love justice? And do I regularly make myself available to others?

While I would love to say that I'm good at doing all of these things and I act perfectly like Jesus on a regular basis, that simply isn't true. I fall short of perfection, I act foolishly, and I don't look like Jesus a lot of the time. But I'm growing little by little every day.

To me, the most beautiful part of all of this is that my growth isn't dependent upon myself. I don't have to strive or force myself to look or act more like Jesus. Instead, it's my job to spend time with Him, love Him, and obey Him—and He'll take care of the rest. I become more like Jesus when I spend time with Him. What a precious gift that is!

Reflection

How do you see wisdom?

Do you share any of the characteristics of wisdom?

What is God saying to you?

DAY 15: PROVERBS 9

Read Proverbs Chapter 9.

What stood out to you in today's Proverb?

Have you ever done something that, at the moment, you thought was brilliant and wise but, in hindsight realized was just foolish? Maybe you invested in a get rich quick scheme that backfired. Or you bought the cheap version of a product only to realize later that you needed the higher quality that came with the more expensive item. Or maybe you made a relational flub that seemed like a great idea at the moment but left you in the proverbial dog house.

It's incredible how wisdom and folly can look so similar in certain instances! When reading through a book like Proverbs, it's easy for us to think of the divide between the two as an enormous chasm, but I think the two are often much closer than we might think. In this Proverb, we catch a glimpse of just how similar wisdom and foolishness can look.

Learning to Spot the Difference

I love wisdom's invitation. First of all, I love bread, especially fresh-baked bread. So I would've been over at Lady Wisdom's house in record time! You would've had to beat me away with a stick to keep me from getting to her delicious feast. Her call is wonderful — it's full of life, hope, and meaning.

The call to foolishness and sin begin the same as wisdom's call. They both call to the "simple" and ask if they're feeling lost. Both claim to be able to solve the problem of confusion, but only one of them can truly follow through on their promise.

Wisdom flourishes in the open.
Sin breeds in secret.

The most significant difference between the two is that one happens out in the open, while the other is hidden. In the story we read today, wisdom leaves her home and goes to the town square that is bustling and full of life. Folly stays at her house, on the front porch, where she can be seen, but just barely. Wisdom asks you to come in for a delicious meal, whereas foolishness is asking you to steal away, without disclosing exactly what will be shared. Wisdom tells you what you can expect, but folly doesn't want to tell you until it's too late.

The truth is that sin usually seems like a good idea at first, but then it takes us further than we want to go and keeps us longer than we wanted to be away. Foolishness is so tempting, but it will, eventually, land us (and others) in a tight spot.

Returning to Wisdom's House

Usually, after I make a foolish mistake, give into sin, or participate in folly, I want to cover it up. I want to creep further into the shadows so no one can see my mistakes. I want to cower in the dark and have a perfect plan ready to fix my image when I reemerge. But this retreat is yet another foolish action.

I think our reactions to our sins and mistakes say a lot about ourselves and what we believe about God. When we sink deeper into the shadows and hide, our actions scream fear. But, if we are sure of God's everlasting and unrelenting love for us, we can run to Him, even when we're frightened, full of regret, or covered in shame. He is wisdom that is beckoning us to the light and away from the shadows. The act of leaving foolishness behind and running to God is the wisest thing we can ever do.

Thankfully, God isn't just wise. He's also gracious. God has buckets and buckets of grace available for us as He, day by day, draws us closer to Himself. He doesn't give up on us when we find ourselves back at folly's house. Instead, He continues to call us back home and back to Himself.

If you've recently found yourself hanging around folly's house, I encourage you to take a step outside of it today. Talk to God, repent of your improper actions, and move closer to Him. Tell someone you trust about your struggles and ask them to hold you accountable as you walk away from sin. Dive deeper into God's word and renew your mind daily as you pursue wisdom in little and big things. It's amazing what God can do when we take a single step!

Reflection

What difference do you see between wisdom and folly?

How can you point others to wisdom's house today?

What is God saying to you?

DAY 16: PROVERBS 9

Read Proverbs Chapter 9.

What stood out to you in today's Proverb?

There's so much goodness in Proverbs 9 that we're going to meditate on this chapter again today!

This chapter highlights the fact that wisdom and folly can look eerily similar, even though they take us down two very different paths. But, smack-dab in the middle of this contrast between wisdom and folly, we find a section of verses that could easily be labeled, "How to Spot a Scoffer 101." In Proverbs 9:7-12, Solomon contrasts how a wise man responds to instruction and how a foolish man reacts to correction. And their actions couldn't be more different.

A foolish man hates correction. He will respond angrily and abusively.

A wise man loves correction. He will respond lovingly. He will apply the instruction to his life.

A foolish man relies on his own strength.

A wise man fears the Lord.

Your response to correction
reveals what you are.

This is the phrase I have scribbled in the margin of my Bible and every time I read it I feel a punch in the heart. My response to correction reveals if I'm wise or foolish and a lot of the time, if I'm honest, I don't like what my answer says about me.

When I'm corrected, I often argue about it. I don't want to be in the wrong. I want to be right at all times. My pride rises within me, and I try to prove wrong the person doing the correcting. I want to point out every one of their flaws, deflect responsibility or do anything I possibly can to ensure that I'm not the one who's getting all of the blame. I don't want to have to change. And have I mentioned that I don't like being wrong?

A wise person once told me to find a kernel of truth in what I'm being confronted with.

Most of the time, I disagree with what I'm being corrected on. But after my initial response of anger and finger-pointing, I try to figure out what I can learn and what I can apply from what they're saying. Even if the person is 80% wrong, I can still choose to take responsibility for my 20%. I think this is where wisdom comes in.

Wisdom is paramount in having a sober self-assessment. Wisdom is responding lovingly in a disagreement. Wisdom is taking loving correction and choosing to change accordingly.

Responding to God's Correction

So far, we've just been focusing on the correction that comes from other people, but how do you respond to God's correction? What do you do when the Holy Spirit prompts you during the middle of a sermon? Or when a specific scripture digs at your heart, revealing a lie you've believed?

I would love to say that I always respond to God's correction promptly and with a happy attitude but that's simply not the case. When He points out a flaw, a sin, or a faulty way of thinking, I usually want to deflect, minimize, or argue it away. I want to shift the blame or ignore Him so that I don't have to change. I want to remain entirely in my comfort zone instead of taking a faith leap of obedience.

Thankfully God lovingly reminds me that I am being corrected because He loves me and wants the best for me. So, after my initial internal temper tantrum, I can quiet my mind and heart and come humbly toward Him. I can lay down my pride because I know that He only corrects those He loves.

What About You?

I've kept today's entry relatively short in the hopes of giving you extra time to reflect on these truths. There's so much value in taking the time to examine how we respond to others and God to determine what these actions reveal about us.

The good news is that we're all works in progress and none of us has this whole following God thing down pat. Today, we can choose to respond more wisely to correction than we did the day before.

Let's seek wisdom today!

Reflection

How do you respond to correction from others? What does that
reveal about you?

How do you respond to God's correction? What does that reveal
about you?

What is God saying to you?

DAY 17: PROVERBS 10

Read Proverbs Chapter 10.

What stood out to you in today's Proverb?

While reading through this Proverb, I was struck by how many times Solomon references speech and the words that we use. I counted 17 times in this one chapter alone. That's a lot of repetition! Clearly, the subject of communication was important to Solomon, and for a good reason—it does affect everything!

What does your speech usually sound like? And what is the speech like of the people around you?

Is there anyone in your life who is always encouraging? They're the cheerleaders in any group, the rays of sunshine, and the ones who are willing to see the glass half full even when you're sure it's half empty.

I wish I were that type of person, but I'm just not.

I'm the one who immediately sees the negative and has to search for the good in things. I enjoy being able to look at the problems in a plan so they can be fixed. If there's something that's wrong, off, or out of place—it's likely I'm going to spot it and fixate upon it. Because this is how my brain works, my speech can become very negative very quickly. It's natural for me to be a Debbie Downer. I have to work to speak life instead of speaking death actively.

Speech is always a reflection of the heart.

Words are some of the best indicators of what's going on inside of our hearts. During times of stress or pressure, if our hearts aren't being guarded and intentionally informed, our language can rapidly become negative. The heart is the wellspring of life and influences everything we say, do, and think.

Wise people measure their words. Fools spout off.

A wise person's speech is worth waiting for. The words of a fool are best ignored.

Words of the wise are full of substance. The speech of fools is full of hot air.

A wise person's speech is a fountain of wisdom. Folly pours out of fools.

Wisdom clears the air. Fools stir up trouble.

Wise speech is intentional, well-timed, and worth listening to.

I wonder how our world would change if we began to measure our speech against this criteria. What if we only spoke intentionally? What if our words were delivered at the right time? And what if we made sure the things we said were worth listening to? That way, no matter if we're frustrated or feeling great, having a light or heavy conversation, encouraging or correcting — we would do it with grace and wisdom.

I want my words to be dripping with wisdom, so those who hear (or read) what I have to say are edified. I want to bring peace to situations using just my words. I don't want to be the one who creates more strife. For me, this means saying less. More and more often in conversations, I'm finding myself falling silent instead of feeling like I need to mention all the words rumbling around in my mind. I'm starting to develop the habit of asking the Lord if it's the right time to say certain things. I'm beginning to read the room to determine if the words I want to say will hurt or help. And I want to limit the number of unhelpful things I say.

I believe that as we tend to our hearts and souls, allowing God to heal and restore, we will see a big difference in our speech. As wisdom and life-giving words begin to flow out of us, I'm sure we will see a drastic change in much of our lives. It's incredible how our speech affects every area of our lives, from home to work to church to our communities. Even interactions with strangers can change if we choose to listen to and speak wisdom regularly.

I long for wise speech to characterize my life. What about you?

Reflection

Do you think your speech lines up with that of wisdom or foolishness?

Based on the state of your speech, what does your heart look like?

What is God saying to you?

DAY 18: PROVERBS 11

Read Proverbs Chapter 11.

What stood out to you in today's Proverb?

I'm writing this chapter in the beginning of November during an election year, so at this particular moment, I'm hyper-aware of the political philosophies of those around me. Election season is one of the few times I hear people discussing values, but even these conversations are just scratching the surface. As believers, our values run so much deeper than a political party and influence our lives so much more than we realize.

Though we talk about them rarely, our value systems pop up in little and big ways throughout our days. Our individual value systems influence our thoughts, words, and actions. What we value affects our relationships, how we spend our time and our money, and how we see the world.

I value comfort, so I'll do things that make me comfortable.

I value work, so I work a lot.

I value excellence, so I want to do things to the best of my abilities.

What Happens When God's Values Differ From Our Own?

Proverbs 11:1 reveals something God values that I don't think is all that big of a deal. The writer tells us that God finds a false balance to be an abomination. He also delights in a just scale.

Abomination? Really, God? That feels a little harsh.
A just scale brings you joy? That seems somewhat odd.

Clearly, my value system differs from God's value system, and only one of us can be right. Since He's God and I'm not, I decided to dig into this verse further in hopes that He would illuminate areas of my thinking that are false.

While God values many things, this verse highlights two things God values very highly: *justice* and *people*.

One of the most amazing characteristics of God is that He is completely just. There's not an ounce of injustice in Him, and He never wavers from justice because it's who He is. True justice is a reflection of His character, and a false scale is nothing short of unjust.

If a scale is unbalanced who gets hurt? *People.*

Who does God love? *People.*

Jesus was the perfect representation of God to us because He is fully God. Because God is just, that means every act of Jesus on this earth was an example of justice for us. He tore down unjust religious systems, loved those who had been oppressed, and proved that justice and mercy are a stunning combination. He also showed us that you can't have justice if you don't have people involved.

Over and over again in the Bible, God commissions His people to act as extensions of Himself and care for those who have been affected by injustice. He instructs us to care for the poor, the orphans, and the widows. He hates injustice because it's not in alignment with who He is and because it hurts those for whom He gave His life. It's simply impossible to extricate true justice from God's everlasting love for people.

Do You Value What God Values?

Honestly, I struggle to care for people. I feel like I'm a thousand times better at dealing with processes than dealing with people. I love my to-do list, and I hate being interrupted. When left to my own devices, I actively avoid relationships and seek opportunities to isolate myself. But this way of thinking doesn't line up with God's character and His ways. And yet, God is patient with me.

When we do have mismatched values (which happens often), He lovingly invites us closer to Himself so He can correct our minds and hearts. He'll put us in situations where our value-system comes into question, and we're forced to line our beliefs up with truth.

For me, the biggest revealer of improper values has been the other godly people I have relationships with. Those are the ones who will lovingly pull me aside and speak truth to me. They're the ones who will invite someone new to sit with them in church and then invite them out to lunch afterward. They're the ones who will ask me how I'm doing and sit with me until I give an honest response. They're the ones who look a lot like Jesus to me when I'm having a rough time. I'm so grateful for those who see the world differently than I do and sometimes, without them even knowing, point me to a different way of thinking and a more godly way of living.

I encourage you to examine your value system today. Put yourself in a position to allow those who love God to speak truth to you as you learn to value the things God loves, together.

Reflection

What does God value that you don't?

Who are the people who remind you of God's values when yours don't match up?

What is God saying to you?

DAY 19: PROVERBS 12

Read Proverbs Chapter 12.

What stood out to you in today's Proverb?

Roots play a vital role in the life and health of a tree, and I think that's exactly what Solomon is inviting us to examine in this Proverb.

When I was seven years old, we had to cut down some Mulberry trees outside my home because they were messing with the foundation of the house. It turns out, the people who planted the trees had no idea just how big the root system would become. Those thirty-year-old trees had withstood so much because of how they were rooted, and we're called to be the same way.

This Proverb focuses on where we're planted, how we spend our time, and with whom we are spending time. So let's tend to our roots!

Where Are You Planted?

Psalm 1 tells us that a righteous person is like a tree that is planted by a steady stream of water. The righteous person will yield good fruit and prosper regardless of the season. Because the person pursuing God is directly connected to the source of life, they will naturally produce the fruit of hope, joy, love, and more. Because their hearts and affections are devoted to Him, they will prosper.

It's so easy to plant ourselves in our careers, our talents, our dreams, or our pasts. We can plant ourselves with our friends, our families, our coworkers, and our church family. These seem like good things, and they are—until they uproot us from our ultimate source, which is God. We're to be rooted and grounded in Him first. From there, our soil makeup might look a little different from person to person. But, ultimately, God is the heavy soil that will nourish us when the storms of life hit and threaten to uproot us.

The Apostle Paul knew just how important being firmly rooted was in the Christian life that he prayed that the church of Ephesus would be rooted and grounded in love (Ephesians 3:17). And Paul's prayer doesn't just apply to the early church—it applies just as much to us today. May we intentionally root ourselves in His love and not uproot ourselves when life gets tough or when things don't go our way.

How Do You Spend Your Time?

Developing strong roots in the right soil doesn't happen overnight. This requires patience and endurance and *sticktoitiveness*. It's the practice of daily choosing to follow God instead of following our natural inclinations. It's opening up our hearts to Him and asking Him to pull out the things that aren't of Him.

For a few friends and me, 2018 was a year of healing, restoration, and intentionally positioning ourselves so God could work in our hearts. We've asked Him to break up the rocky soil, pull up unhealthy roots, and plant us in places where we will prosper. But this is a time-consuming process. It requires us to individually sit with Him and put in hard work. A lot of hard *heart* work. Some of the fruit has popped up right away while other fruit has taken a little longer.

Proverbs 12 talks about the righteous not being uprooted, which sounds great, but we don't get to see the process by which the righteous grow so secure. Deeply rooted trees are only that way because of the growth over years or decades that happened beneath the surface. It's the firm foundation cultivated over time that makes a person or a tree able to stand firm in the midst of a storm. Deep, secure roots in the proper soil can lead to a flourishing tree and a beautiful life.

How Do You Choose Your Company?

The people we choose to surround ourselves with is the third group I think Solomon is inviting us to examine. In sticking with the tree metaphor, each tree is part of the overall ecosystem, and they all contribute to the state of the area. If a tree is hogging too much water, the others are deprived. If it's soaking up more than its share of the nutrients from the soil, the others will go hungry.

Do you have any people like that in your life? People, who suck the life out of you? Or those who encourage you to follow anyone other than the Lord? What about the ones who always speak harshly or negatively to you?

Conversely, who are the people who speak life to you and point you to God and His goodness? Who tells you who you are in Christ even when you don't believe it yourself? Who reminds you of what true life looks like?

I would encourage you to reach out to those who give you life today and deepen those relationships. Spend some extra time in the Word and with God today. Choose to tend to your roots, giving your spirit what it needs to grow and flourish!

Reflection

What does your root system look like?

How can you spend more time this week deepening your roots in Jesus?

What is God saying to you?

DAY 20: PROVERBS 13

Read Proverbs Chapter 13.

What stood out to you in today's Proverb?

I don't remember much of my childhood, but I distinctly remember one thing: giving a lot of advice. As early as second grade, I remember friends coming to me, asking me what they should do in a given situation. We would spend our recess walking the perimeter of our elementary school's field discussing their problem. Then, about three quarters of the way around the field, I would tell them what I thought was best.

Oddly enough, this trend is still the same today (just without the grass and bugs). I have many people who come to me looking for advice on a variety of subjects. In my 20+ years since those mini-counseling sessions, I've learned that I don't like giving advice anymore. I used to tell people what they should do, but my motivations were never wholly pure.

Looking back, part of my motivation for advice-giving was to make myself feel smart or superior. I took immense pride in being the one with all the answers. Now I realize that my giving advice was more about me than them, though they likely had no idea about my internal heart posture.

Today, instead of giving advice, I like to create safe spaces for people to talk and, 90% of the time, they can arrive at a solution that will work for them on their own, with little interference from me. And that's so much more fun!

Now I know I can simply create safe, transparent spaces and God will bring the healing.

What Are You Bringing With You?

It's so easy to pick up baggage and distractions along the way and become focused on ourselves, our situations, or a hundred other things. When I'm connected to the Lord, I bring health and wisdom to situations. When I'm relying on my strength, I become prideful and self-focused—two of folly's defining characteristics.

"A wicked messenger falls into trouble,

but a trustworthy envoy brings healing."

Proverbs 13:17

I don't know about you, but I don't want to be labeled as a "wicked messenger," and I most assuredly don't want to fall into trouble. Instead, I want to be known as trustworthy. I want to be a person who can bring healing to any situation. How about you?

The word "healing" in the Hebrew refers to a refreshing of the body and the mind. As ambassadors of Christ (2 Corinthians 5:20) and representatives of His Kingdom, we can bring light to darkness, hope to doubt, and combat lies with truth. Guided by the Holy Spirit, we can speak life when there is death and become the conduit for refreshment that the world so desperately needs.

How powerful is that? God can move through us—changing someone's situation, perspective, and life!

If you want refreshing and healing to be indicative of your life, I encourage you to ask God if He will use you in this way. After all, He is a good Father who gives good gifts to His children. Ask to experience that healing in your own life and then ask for opened eyes so you can be refreshing to someone else.

A few years ago, I intentionally prayed that I would be a peace-bringer to chaotic situations and, it happened! I was put into some stressful and crazy situations and was able to be a conduit for the peace of God to flow in that place. And, if He did it in my life, I'm sure He will do it for you. You only need to ask.

Let's be so full of Him that we bring healing and refreshment to those we encounter. And let's pray for open eyes to the opportunities around us today!

Reflection

What do you bring with you wherever you go? Have you picked up any baggage you need to offload?

Do you believe you're an Ambassador of Christ? How are you living that out?

What is God saying to you?

DAY 21: PROVERBS 14

Read Proverbs Chapter 14.

What stood out to you in today's Proverb?

Are there any verses that stand out to you every time you read the Bible? Proverbs 14:4 is one of those verses for me!

"Where there are no oxen, the manger is clean,

but abundant crops come by the strength of the ox."

Proverbs 14:4

This seems like such a random verse in the middle of some really profound teaching on wisdom. What does farming have to do with being wise? What do crops have to do with not speaking foolishly?

While I can come up with some correlations between farm life and wisdom, I think Solomon is drawing attention to our priorities yet again. Solomon understood the reality that every choice we make has ramifications.

If your main concern is a clean barn, you should get rid of your oxen who are notoriously messy creatures.

If your main concern is having enough food to eat, you need to use your oxen and incur the inconvenience of a messy barn.

What are you primarily concerned about?
How are those concerns influencing your decisions?

Over the years, I have developed the habit of self-protection. It is my primary concern in many different areas of my life. Years ago, I took on the role of being my own personal protector—a role that was never mine to take on. I even have a hard time trusting God to protect me because it's so ingrained in my mind and heart that I need to defend myself. Because this is my focus, many of my decisions are based on this need.

Because self-protection is my priority, I've missed out on a lot of things in my life.

People are the ones who can hurt me, so I tend to isolate myself from others.

Isolation is dreary, so I fill my time with plenty of distractions, like work and comfort, so I don't get bored.

When I meet a new person, I'm sure they're going to hurt me, so I don't let them in.

I seek ways to mitigate risk, limit my exposure to pain, and remove opportunities for hurt.

But the truth is this: if we want to accomplish anything significant in this life, there's going to be expense, mess, and inconvenience.

Jesus Was Inconvenienced

Jesus was inconvenienced constantly by the people who wanted something from Him. How many times was Jesus interrupted on His way to another city or town? How often was He pulled away from a prayer by the needs of those around Him? If Jesus had valued His convenience over His mission, we would be utterly hopeless and without a Savior.

Jesus Embraced The Mess

You don't have to look very far to see just how messy the world around us is. We've polluted the earth, filled the oceans with garbage, and turned much of the land into a concrete jungle. But, more than that, people are messy. Being in relationships with other flawed humans is messy. They're going to say things that hurt you, and you're going to do things that hurt them. You'll annoy each other, frustrate each other, and peeve each other. But relationships are vital. We weren't made to be alone—we're created to embrace the mess as Jesus did.

Jesus Incurred The Expense

God bankrupted heaven when He sent Jesus to earth. He incurred the greatest expense in the history of the universe to bring us back into right relationship with Him! The price of our sin was so great that Jesus paid for it with His life and death. He accepted our debt and gave us His life in return. His priorities were set on one thing: us. We were so valuable to Him that He was willing to give His best for us!

I believe that as we walk with God, our priorities will begin to line up with His and our hearts will start to beat in sync with His own. The more time we spend with Him, the more we'll become like Him. You might not want to incur any inconvenience, mess, or expense right now — and that's okay, I'm right there with you. We have the privilege of spending the rest of our lives growing in this area and becoming more like Him!

I encourage you to start today; do something inconvenient for someone in your life and see what happens!

Reflection

What do your priorities look like?

Are you willing to embrace the expense, messiness, and inconvenience that comes with following Christ? Why or why not?

What is God saying to you?

DAY 22: PROVERBS 15

Read Proverbs Chapter 15.

What stood out to you in today's Proverb?

I love the show Jeopardy. As a kid, one of my dreams was to be a contestant on the show, even if I didn't win. I would watch it with my grandma in the middle of the day and erupt with joy every time I would get an answer right. I would always announce triumphantly, "I just won $200!" — thrilled that my smarts could result in a payday. While I no longer have a desire ever to be a contestant, I still have an insatiable thirst for knowledge.

No matter how much knowledge I acquire, I'll never know as much as God.

Have you ever thought about the amount of knowledge God has? He is all-knowing, and nothing gets by Him. He knows what happened a thousand years ago and knows exactly what's going to take place a thousand years from now. Each plant, animal, and human is under God's purview. He knows the time the sun will rise and set each day and the number of stars, planets, and galaxies that exist.

More than that, He knows each of us! And the walls we put up between Him and us do us no good — He still knows it all! Every thought, feeling, action, inkling, and desire are laid out plainly before Him. He knows every good thing and every bad thing, each moment of jealousy and act of kindness, all the deep, dark secrets, all the stuff we shout from the rooftops, and everything in between.

This characteristic of God used to scare me. Partially because I can't comprehend a being who can know all of that, but mostly because I wasn't sure what He would do with all that intimate knowledge of me. I've been rejected by others when they've learned too much, mocked after sharing something deep and personal, and been gossiped about after a moment of transparency. And, for many years, I let these negative past experiences with people color my view of God.

God never uses His knowledge of us against us.

This baffles me! God has so much ammo He could use against me! He could easily take the sin I don't want to admit and guilt trip me for all eternity. He could weaponize the dirt He has on me and employ it to manipulate me into obedience. He could shame me, reinforcing the lies I already believe about myself.

But He would never do that.

God knows every single thing about us, and He still chooses us. His love isn't based on our performance, it's based on His character—and that's something that will never change. Though we are fickle human beings who will reject wisdom and even reject God, He patiently waits, drawing us back to Himself time and time again.

We are never too far gone for His love, and He passionately pursues us, even when we're sprinting away from Him.

Because His love is true love—without shame, guilt, manipulation, fear, or insecurity—we can come to Him and lay ourselves bare before Him. Though He already knows everything, He celebrates those moments when we come openly and honestly to Him, tearing down the protective barriers we've erected over the years. He gives us the courage to tear these walls down, sometimes brick by brick, and other times with a wrecking ball, so we'll experience a deeper level of intimacy with Him.

Have You Experienced This Before?

Currently, I'm learning the beautiful freedom that comes from daily confession. I'm amazed at the love I feel when I lay my soul bare before the Lord. It's wildly uncomfortable and, at first, I don't like it all that much, but the results are well worth the momentary discomfort.

And I still have a long way to go in this area. I look forward to the day when I'll sprint to Him instead of running away first. I'm thankful that He's patiently leading me one step at a time as I learn to honor Him and walk with Him.

Today's Proverb reminds me that our God has infinite knowledge of me (even the things I don't tell Him) and He still loves me the same. Nothing can change how He feels about me and the same is true for you.

Reflection

How do you feel about God's intimate knowledge of you?

How can you share more of yourself with Him today?

What is God saying to you?

DAY 23: PROVERBS 16

Read Proverbs Chapter 16.

What stood out to you in today's Proverb?

Whenever I pick a specific book of the Bible to focus on and write about, I realize just how little I know about that book. I feel like I always stumble upon verses I didn't know were there. It's as if they had been hiding, lying in wait until the right time for me to see them. Proverbs 16:7 is one of those verses. I feel like, for years, I was so focused on the verses all around it, that I missed this precious gem. So let's dig in to the two main components of this fantastic verse.

The Pleasure of The Lord

Do you believe that God is pleased with you? If you've placed your trust in Jesus, then He is pleased with you! Which is absolutely amazing! The Almighty God, the Creator of the universe who knows everything about you, takes pleasure in *you*. We don't have to do anything for God to be pleased with us, just like we don't have to do anything to earn God's love. He is perfectly pleased with Jesus, and He now sees us through His perfect sacrifice.

The truth is, we can't please God without faith (Hebrews 11:6). It's not through works, striving, or some behavior modification program but a heart posture. I think this is why the heart is emphasized so strongly throughout the book of Proverbs—our heart is vital to our relationship with God. He wants our hearts.

Our hearts get banged up and bruised throughout our lives. We can make stupid mistakes and disappoint those whose opinions we value the most. We can be careless and hurt someone else, leading to their displeasure. We can fall from grace or fail so spectacularly that how others see us is completely changed. And, if that happens enough or for long enough, we can begin to see ourselves as achieving machines who find their identities in what we do rather than who we are in Him.

We can so easily transfer our performance-based relationships onto God. But that's not at all how it works. He loved us when we had nothing to offer, sacrificed Himself for us before we had a chance to choose Him, and called us "children" when we were still acting out and running away.

His pleasure is based on our position as his kids, not on our performance. And because our identity as children is secure in Jesus, we can feel confident in the truth contained in the second half of this verse.

Making Peace with Enemies

The Bible is full of examples of people who were opposed to one another. It seems like almost every major Bible character had a significant enemy they were combatting at some point in their lives. These struggles often seem impossible to mend, but with God, result in supernatural reunification.

Jacob and Esau were brothers who took the concept of sibling rivalry to a whole new level. Jacob stole his brother's birthright and was forced to flee because Esau vowed to kill him. Then, just a few chapters later in Genesis 33, the two brothers reconciled. The person who was once Jacob's enemy made peace with him!

Joseph's brothers loathed him so much that they tried to kill him (talk about dysfunction!). They threw him into a pit, sold him into slavery, and started him on the path that would lead him to be wrongfully imprisoned, forgotten, and then eventually to running the nation of Egypt. In Genesis 50, we see the goodness of God in Joseph's response to his brothers who had mistreated him so severely. Joseph could've held a grudge, and he could've "gotten even." Instead, he decided to respond humbly and kindly to those who had wronged him the most.

In 2 Corinthians 5, Paul tells us that we've been reconciled to God, so we should reconcile with others. Because of Christ's sacrifice, the sin that separated us from Him has been demolished, eliminating the distance between us. We are called, as His children, to do the same with the people in our lives. We carry the ministry of reconciliation with us and take it wherever we go.

The good news is, like everything else in this life, we don't have to do this alone. Living peaceably with others isn't entirely dependent on us. God gives us the desire and the help we need to live this out. In the lives of Jacob and Joseph, the Lord was changing their hearts while He was working on the lives of those they had wronged or those who had done wrong to them. This way, when the opportunity for peace presented itself, they were able to embrace it and those who had once been enemies became true brothers.

We don't have to love our enemies to please God but we can go out on a limb because we know His pleasure is secured. His love for us isn't connected to the result of the conversation or the state of the relationship at the end. Instead, His love remains consistent and true no matter what. And, because we have first been reconciled to Him, we can live peaceably with all, to the best of our ability (Romans 12:18).

Reflection

Do you believe God is pleased with you? Why or why not?

How are you intentionally living peaceably with those around you?

What is God saying to you?

DAY 24: PROVERBS 17

Read Proverbs Chapter 17.

What stood out to you in today's Proverb?

Have you ever experienced moments or seasons where you were under immense pressure? Like when your car is in the shop, you're under the weather, and your boss is breathing down your neck all on the same day. Or that long-lasting constant pressure that accompanies a bout with illness, a stretch of unemployment, or struggling to fit in when everyone around you seems to click easily.

Those are the seasons I believe the Lord is testing our hearts to see what's going to come out of them. It's like what happened to the character Job in the Bible. When everything was taken away from him (other than his nagging wife and his miserable group of friends), he had plenty of opportunities to blame, curse, or turn his back on God. But he didn't. He still loved God and remained committed to Him during the absolute worst time in his life. Though he might have been tempted, and though he was strongly encouraged to do so by his friends—he never cursed God. When his heart was tested, he was still completely faithful.

What comes from your heart when it's tested?

In Proverbs 17:3, our hearts are compared to silver and gold and God's testing is likened to a furnace. These metals in and of themselves, without the fiery furnace, have little value. These alloys only become precious when they go through the fire. Without the fire, there is little value.

This topic of the refining fire is seen throughout the Bible. God has always put His children in the crucible; and I believe He does this to show us and others who He is and who we are in Him. During a difficult time, if you're able to react in peace instead of strife like you used to, you will see a difference in yourself—and others likely will too. If you're kind to the person who hurt you instead of screaming at them, that'll show some serious heart change!

It's amazing how God's goodness and grace toward us can be

seen more easily in the midst of difficulty. In those moments, we learn what we're made of and who He's called us to be. This doesn't lessen the discomfort but can help us maintain a broader perspective when we're in the midst of a less-than-favorable situation.

What blows me away about God is that he purchased my heart before it was worth anything. It was hard and broken and bitter. There was no hope of getting anything worthwhile out of it. But he paid the most precious ransom for my heart before I had a chance to accept Him. He had already gone all-in for me, giving me the opportunity to reject Him (something I did, without remorse, for many years).

Though it doesn't feel good, the fire is the most loving thing He could do because it's not meant to destroy but to refine us. By testing our hearts, we can see what's precious inside of us.

The State of The Heart

A hard heart produces wicked speech, lies, and mockery. It leads to the mistreatment of others and severs relationships. This changes perspectives, making evil "good" and good "evil," which eventually leads to a misunderstanding of true judgment.

It's when I snap at the person who gave me bad news or I'm filled with jealousy when someone gets something I think I deserve. It's those moments when I am so uncomfortable in my circumstances that I seek comfort and joy in things instead of God. It's those times when I isolate from others because I don't want to risk getting hurt again.

On the other hand, a heart that's being refined seeks and values wisdom. From it flows words that are joyful, life-giving, and encouraging. This leads to thriving relationships that stick close, even during hard times.

It's in the times I choose to trust God when things seem to be going sideways or say, "not my will, but yours be done," when circumstances are outside of my control. Or those moments when I serve someone else instead of being selfish or choose humility over pride. It's when I confess, repent, or apologize when I've sinned and hurt someone else.

The beautiful part of this life is that we're never going to be perfect. Our hearts will always have some junk in them that need to be refined and removed. But each moment in the furnace of circumstance is an invitation to grow and see the gold hidden within our hearts.

How Do You See The Fiery Furnace?

Every circumstance, unwelcome interaction, or piece of bad news, is an opportunity to examine our hearts and see what's lurking below the surface. It's an invitation to see what is in our hearts that can only be exposed during the hard times. The truth is, it doesn't always feel like something life-giving—sometimes it feels like an unwelcome beatdown. Whether good or bad, our perspective on the fiery furnace influences how we react to God's refining process.

If you're in the refining fire right now, I encourage you to cling even more tightly to God. Believe it or not, He is right in the thick of it with you. Reach out to a few godly people and ask them to pray for you and support you as you walk through this season.

If you're not in a refining season, my guess is that you probably know someone who is. I encourage you to reach out to them today and commit to praying for them. Encourage them, speak life to them, meet practical needs, and be a shoulder to cry on. Let's be the kind of friends who love at all times, even when it's inconvenient for us.

Reflection

Do you see your heart as precious?

How do you react when you're in the refining fire?

What is God saying to you?

DAY 25: PROVERBS 18

Read Proverbs Chapter 18.

What stood out to you in today's Proverb?

Have you ever heard the quote, "Your mouth is writing checks your body can't cash"? There are many colorful variations of this phrase, but they all mean virtually the same thing: a person is talking a big game on which they can't follow through.

It's the person who embellishes the skills on their resume but, when push comes to shove, can't really speak German or create a pivot table. It's the salesperson who brags about this incredible new product, only for it to be a lemon. It's the friend who doesn't want you to be single, so they talk up the blind date they've set you up with—leaving you to find out that he's far from Bruce Wayne.

Today's Proverb is full of people who talk a big talk but aren't able to walk it out. And this chapter tells us precisely what pride leads to: a fall.

Have you ever experienced this?

Over the past few weeks, I have watched several people, whose skills took them to a place their character couldn't keep them, fall from places of honor. Each of these instances led to truly spectacular fallouts. These people, though well-intentioned, had overestimated their skills and underestimated their character. Then, instead of owning their mistakes, they lashed out because of hurt, exposing even further the state of their hearts.

I'm pretty sure we've all been in this situation before. I know I have. I was let go from a job simply because my character sucked. Though I had all the skills necessary for the position, at the end of the day, I was a jerk and treated people terribly so I didn't deserve to work there any longer. Of course, I didn't see this years ago when it happened. I was filled with pride and was crushed when I was confronted with the truth. Now, looking back, being let go was the most loving thing my bosses could've done for me. And now, I'm incredibly grateful for it. Being fired was the wakeup call I needed to take a good, long look at the state of my heart.

Humility Begets Honor

Proverbs 18:16 reminds us that we don't need to boast or inflate our accolades and greatness, but that our skills will make room for us. The God-given gifts we've taken the time to hone are the ones that bring us into places of influence. We can gain access to some pretty incredible sites, but the key to staying in those places of authority comes a few lines earlier in verse 12.

"...humility comes before honor."

Proverbs 18:12

If we want to be honored, we need to first humble ourselves. And I'm not talking about being meek, shy or unsure of ourselves—self-deprecation is *not* humility. Instead, humility is knowing who you are and who God is. It's knowing that our skills come from God alone and aren't something that we drum up on our own. Humility believes what God says about us.

Before we can be honored, we first have to honor others, even if we feel like they don't deserve it. We're called to respect others, no matter their gifts, position, or title. We're created to serve others, even when we don't have to or want to. So let's position ourselves to celebrate others, especially if they have similar gifts to ours.

The truth is this: seeing, loving, and celebrating others doesn't diminish your gifts or skills—it shows your character and the goodness of God. Taking the spotlight off yourself shows that you're so secure in who you are and who God has called you to be that you don't need to hoard the attention. You don't need to barge onto center stage or scream and stomp your feet until you get what you want. But you know, that by honoring others, you'll receive honor in due time.

This life of humility and honoring others isn't something that comes overnight. It's not something I think we'll ever master, but it is, without question, the way we're called to live. There's nothing more attractive than someone who is humble and honors those around them!

Today, let's find one practical way to leave the exaggerations at home and pick up humility instead!

Reflection

Do you ever write checks your body can't cash? Why?

How are you displaying humility in your daily life? How can you humble yourself today?

What is God saying to you?

DAY 26: PROVERBS 19

Read Proverbs Chapter 19.

What stood out to you in today's Proverb?

Recently, I discussed with a friend just how difficult wealth management must be for the ultra-wealthy. Now, I'm not talking about having to choose which Lamborghini you want to drive around town that morning, but the real struggles that come with a having a great deal of wealth: paying taxes, making enough to cover the taxes, knowing where all your money is in different bank accounts (because you can't just have one), not to mention all of the people who come out of the woodwork wanting something from you once you have wealth. Can you imagine never trusting the people in your life, always wondering if someone is befriending you just for the money? It sounds like a lonely way of life.

While most of us likely don't share the problems of the ultra-rich, we all have assets we've been given. Some are rich monetarily, others relationally, some are incredibly skilled, and others have more ideas than they know what to do with. No matter what we have in what quantity, we are responsible for stewarding these assets well.

How are you using the assets you've been given?

Money is a subject we hate talking about in any religious context, and, if you're an American, there's a good chance you hate talking about money in almost any setting. If that's you, get ready to be uncomfortable, because we're about to talk about money.

I believe your habits with money reflect your value system. If you value yourself, you're going to spend money on yourself. If you value a particular person (especially if you're in a dating relationship), you're going to treat them to things. If you value security, you're going to save, save, and save some more. If you trust God with your money, you'll be willing to give to Him (even when funds are tight).

But everything isn't about money.

What gifts have you been given? Are you administrative, creative, or supportive? Are you a great leader or follower? Do you have skills that set you apart from your colleagues or peers? Is there something you do that's easy for you, yet hard for someone else? Those are all gifts you've been given and deserve to be stewarded well.

I'm discovering that relationships are one of the most critical commodities in this world. I'm in no way saying that we should use the people in our lives, in fact, I'm saying the exact opposite. Let us value the relationships we've been given because there's nothing in this world quite like healthy and life-giving relationships.

As an introverted and task-oriented person, I tend to get caught up in tasks and processes instead of focusing on people. To counter this natural tendency of mine, I have to continually remind myself that Jesus loves and died for people — not my to-do list. And, even though it stretches me outside my comfort zone, when I'm intentionally using my gifts to serve others, I feel more like my real self.

The way we treat our relationships reveals how we view God and ourselves.

Have you ever taken the time to consider that you are an incredible asset? God loves and died for you. Without you, you can't gain wealth, have relationships, or have any ideas, vision, or plans. You really are amazing! You have been entrusted with your heart, soul, mind, and strength and you are called to use what you have well.

I haven't always had a great view of myself — I am overcoming things like doubt, insecurity, and even self-hatred. I'm learning to replace those old ways of thinking and choosing to value myself because God values me. Taking care of me is an act of obedience, trust, and faith. My heart, soul, mind, and strength have been entrusted to me by the God who loves me, and I need to steward *me* well.

I encourage you to really take a look at how you're using your assets. If you identify an area that has some room for improvement, celebrate that and invite God to help you. He is ready and willing to help us when we call out to Him!

Reflection

Is there an asset that you know you aren't stewarding well? What's one thing you can do this week to improve that?

Based on how you treat your assets, what do you value?

What is God saying to you?

DAY 27: PROVERBS 20

Read Proverbs Chapter 20.

What stood out to you in today's Proverb?

In January 2017 I made the conscious decision to stop drinking alcohol *before* my habit became a problem. I wasn't allowing myself to get drunk. I wasn't drinking every day, and, according to many people, I didn't have a problem. But I did. The truth is that I was thinking about drinking every day. Every. Single. Day. Within an hour or two of sitting down at my desk, I would be thinking about just how badly I wanted (or needed) a beer or something stronger. In my mind, drinking was the best way for me to solve my problems. Alcohol was the solution I desired even though I rarely acted upon my craving. Instead of praying, talking with trusted counsel, or other healthy forms of stress relief — I controlled, I complained, and I fantasized about drinking.

Though I wasn't getting drunk, I was still under the influence of alcohol.

When I was reading through today's Proverb, I was struck by the many different things we can be influenced by — and this isn't even an exhaustive list! I encourage you to read back through the chapter and see how many different external forces, internal character traits, and deep desires can influence and even control us. It is eye-opening!

External Influence

Are there any substances that have control over you?
Are there any cravings that augment how you live your life?

If so, you might have an addiction of some sort. It might be to food, television, social media, or the traditional addictions we're used to hearing about like alcohol and drugs. While the writer of this Proverb only calls out alcohol, many other substances can end up controlling our behavior. And, when some external substance controls us, we're not being controlled by the Spirit (Ephesians 5:18).

Again, God isn't after some behavior modification program —

He's after our hearts. If some other substance is controlling us, then there's at least a part of us that's not under the influence of the Spirit. God wants our whole hearts and lives because that's how He created us to live.

Internal Influence

There are many different internal motivations listed in this Proverb—laziness, greed, pride, and vengeance to name a few. As children of God, none of these should drive us, and yet, so often they do. We see this when we spend an entire weekend binge-watching tv or ignore spending time with God in order to make another buck. It's those times when we puff ourselves up or when we get even with someone else. These actions are all a result of an internal heart posture that isn't entirely in line with who God is and who we are. These actions are all outside the character of friends of God.

Just as we've been discussing from the beginning, these internal motivations are matters of the heart that God wants to heal. By nature, we will fall into dysfunction and pursue things other than God. But that's why we're called to inform our hearts and renew our minds. We are to meditate on the characteristics of God (Philippians 4:8) and turn our affections toward Him.

Each negative internal motivation reveals that our priorities are out of order and are due for a reordering.

Godly Influence

I love that not all hope is lost in this chapter. We can be under the influence of the things of God like righteousness, love, faithfulness, and more! But, we don't muster up these attributes on our own. Each comes as a result of spending time with Him. As we seek His word, His face, and His will, we can put away the external and internal influences that no longer serve us in order to take up those He's called us to. We can daily choose to live more like Him and less like who we used to be.

This is a beautiful and challenging process. We don't need to have it all figured out right now. We just need to take a single step forward. That might look like having a quiet time every day before the rest of the house wakes. Or going to a 12-step meeting in your area. Or sharing the secret that's tearing you up with a trusted person to help you process. Or it could be a thousand other things, but I believe the Holy Spirit will highlight what you need to do next. My hope and prayer are that each of us will have the courage to take the next step that He's leading us to.

You can do it!

Reflection

What's influencing you? List both the good and the bad.

What's one practical thing you can do (or stop doing) today to put yourself under the influence of God, eliminating the power of the bad?

What is God saying to you?

DAY 28: PROVERBS 21

Read Proverbs Chapter 21.

What stood out to you in today's Proverb?

As I'm writing this, my church is going through a year-long series called "Rooted in Jesus." The idea is that when we get rooted in Jesus, we can flourish in life. And, if we're not rooted in Jesus, or if our roots are shallow, then we can never be the people He's called us to be or do the things He's called us to do. This means that before we can focus on doing all kinds of amazing things with and for God, we have to first sit, be still, and learn who we are and who He is. One of the many things I've loved about this series is that we've done regular check-ups. Every quarter we have a "Rooted Checkpoint" where we'll take an entire service to stop and evaluate where we're at individually. That's it. We pause for a moment of quiet introspection to take a realistic look at how we're doing. The truth is, if we don't know how we're doing then we can't take the necessary steps to improve.

Today we're going to stop and check in with ourselves.

I encourage you to pause for a moment and ask the Holy Spirit what He's saying to you right now. Then sit in silence for a few moments and wait for Him to speak. Take the time to write down what He's saying to you.

God is Bigger Than Our Motivations

There can be a million motivations for our actions, and this Proverb covers quite a few of them. In this chapter alone, I see pride, greed, impatience, ignorance, busyness, and comfort. These internal forces, and many more that aren't listed, can drive us to unhealthy, dishonoring, or unproductive behaviors.

Despite all of these heart issues, God still loves us. He chose a relationship with you and me knowing full well the wrong things drive us. He desires a relationship with us though we consistently seek pleasure and fulfillment in worldly pleasures rather than in Him. And, as we continue to pursue Him, we'll experience His conviction when our hearts don't line up with His perfect standard.

Just before sitting down to write this section, I was convicted about a text message I recently sent. Though there was nothing wrong with the content, I intentionally sent it outside of a group text because I wanted to talk to this person separate from a mutual friend. It's subtle and, as I'm writing this, doesn't "seem like a big deal," but it's a big deal to God and me. He cares so deeply about our motivations. He honestly does weigh the heart.

If you've felt conviction at any point during your Bible reading or through this devotional, that's something to celebrate. God convicts His children and redirects those He loves. Conviction is that bittersweet nudge from our perfect and loving Father because He cares for us. If you've felt convicted, lean into that, thank the Lord, ask for forgiveness, and welcome Him into that unhealthy part of your heart that chose something over Him. Ask Him to heal those broken pieces and pray for the courage to walk in a way that's worthy of being called a child of God. I pray that we would be able to hear Him clearly as we set aside time to listen to His voice today.

Reflection

How's your heart?

What improper motivation do you need to submit to God and allow Him to heal?

What is God saying to you?

DAY 29: PROVERBS 22

Read Proverbs Chapter 22.

What stood out to you in today's Proverb?

What are you passionate about?

I bet if you were to list out your passions, there would be more than a few of them because we are passionate people! We're passionate because God is passionate and we're made in His image. We can love, enjoy, and experience wondrous things because we're like our heavenly Father.

One fundamental truth this Proverb reminds me of is that God is a compassionate God. He loves people so profoundly and consistently draws people to Himself. His love knows no bounds and never stops pursuing people. But there is one group God demonstrates His love explicitly toward: the poor.

Throughout the Bible, God brings our attention to the poor, reminding those with abundance not to forget them. In both the Old and New Testaments, God makes a point to let us know He cherishes the impoverished. God is passionate about the poor because He's passionate about *all* people, without discrimination.

It's easy to think of "the poor" as people who are struggling financially. You might think of the homeless or those in Section 8 housing—but there are so many other forms of poverty:

monetary

relational

spiritual

physical

emotional

mental

and more.

A PROVERB A DAY

"Whoever has a bountiful eye will be blessed,

for he shares his bread with the poor."

Proverbs 22:9

According to the footnote in my Bible, the word used for "bountiful" can also be translated as "good," which makes this verse all the more interesting to me.

If you have a good eye — because your body is healthy and full of light (Luke 11:34-36) — then you will be blessed. Because we know that faith without works is dead (James 2:14-26), we know that our goodness should be evident. In the midst of darkness, light is apparent — it can't be missed. If we are being redeemed and transformed by God from the inside out, we will naturally be sharing with those who lack. It's not a box we have to check off as part of our religious duties or something we do during the holidays to appease our guilt. It should be a natural outpouring of the life and work of Christ in us.

When we look at this through the lens of the New Testament, it gets even better! Jesus said He is the bread of life (John 6:35), which means we're not just to give money or food to the poor, but we're tasked to share Jesus with those who find themselves lacking. No matter the lack, we can always point people back to Jesus, the Creator and Sustainer of everything. And, what I love about Jesus is that a lot of the time, we can act like Him without ever having to say His name.

When we sit with someone in the hospital when they're sick, we're sharing Jesus with them.

When we welcome a new person to the neighborhood, we're showing love as Jesus did.

When we spend time with the imprisoned, we are shining His light in the darkness.

When we cry with the heartbroken, we are giving them a glimpse of God.

Imagine what the world would look like if we deliberately spent time each week sharing Jesus, the Bread of Life, with those who were lacking. What if we did this in little ways with our families, friends, neighbors, coworkers, and total strangers? What if we truly were the hands and feet of Jesus, bringing life and love to a dark and hurting world?

I think that sounds like a pretty awesome way to live. Let's try it out this week!

Reflection

In what areas are you poor? In what areas are you rich?

How can you share Jesus with the poor this week?

What is God saying to you?

DAY 30: PROVERBS 23

Read Proverbs Chapter 23.

What stood out to you in today's Proverb?

For years, I've taught kids and adults, both in and outside the church, through the written word and in-person teaching. I love being able to be part of the learning process and helping others go from not knowing to knowing. One of the main things I've learned about teaching is that repetition is a valuable tool to utilize. If the lesson we're attempting to understand is continuously in front of us, and if we hear about it over and over again, no matter our age, we're going to be more likely to remember it.

God made us and knows this important fact about how our brains and hearts work. Because of this, He strategically laid out His Word so we can read and understand what He's communicating to us. God's use of repetition as a literary tool is so intentional. The repeated words and phrases are the ones the Almighty really wants to sink in. He doesn't say anything to fill a word quota and He doesn't repeat any phrase by accident.

In Proverbs 22 and again in Proverbs 23 the writer commands against rezoning and the moving of landmarks. At first, I asked the Lord why He made such a big deal about this, but after some research, this text took on a whole new meaning.

"Do not move an ancient landmark or enter the fields of the fatherless,

for their Redeemer is strong; he will plead their cause against you."

Proverbs 23:10-11

The ancient landmarks were boundaries that had been set out many years before to clearly mark whose land belonged to who. These landmarks carried a deep financial meaning and a profound implication for the inheritance of future generations.

Imagine that you owned a beautiful piece of land that had been in your family for many years. You and your family were comfortable there and spent time making the house and surrounding area feel like home. You had a garden and a tire swing or a wrap-around porch and a tree fort or whatever elements you envision as part of your perfect house. Incurring a substantial expense, you recently had a pool and a jacuzzi installed — the cherry on top of your dream house. One night, you went to bed, feeling satisfied and excited to finally utilize these new features with your family the next day. But when you woke in the morning you discovered your beautiful pool was now blocked by an ugly fence — your neighbor's fence. They had moved their boundary line and were now claiming that the pool and jacuzzi were theirs. They had just stolen your property and a piece of the inheritance you were going to pass on to your children.

This isn't an exact parallel, but I hope you get the point. The moving of an ancient landmark would be similar to a situation where your neighbor moved their fence and tried to take your property. This was deceitful, an act of theft, and just plain wrong. More than that, the moving of ancient landmarks often happened to widows and orphans, those who were unable to defend themselves because they had no one to plead their case. They didn't have a defender, so they were the easiest to pick off — or so some thought.

What the thieves or boundary movers didn't realize was that God was the one who would redeem what had been taken. They had no idea that the Lord is a protector of His children and has a knack for turning even the worst scenarios into good for His people. The truth is that God still redeems what has been lost today. We all started as spiritual orphans who didn't know what to do with our boundary lines. We misused talents, used people, and even abused ourselves because we simply didn't know any better. We lived separated from our Father, serving only ourselves and our desires. We weren't complete or whole, we were abandoned and alone, and we hid from God instead of running to Him. Still He redeemed us.

God so graciously took our identities from orphaned and alone to children of God. He saw us in our mess and still sought to save us and bring us into right relationship with Him. Through Him, we now have access to all good things, and Jehovah withholds nothing good from us. We are children of the King, and our inheritance is Christ Himself. He is the most beautiful gift we can ever receive, and it's one that can never be taken away from us.

The cross is an ancient landmark that cannot be moved, and for that, I am immensely grateful.

Reflection

How have you seen God as the Redeemer in your life?

What does it mean to you to have Christ as your inheritance?

What is God saying to you?

DAY 31: PROVERBS 24

Read Proverbs Chapter 24.

What stood out to you in today's Proverb?

I love asking other Christians what their favorite Bible verse is because I feel like it always says so much about who they are, what they value, and how they see the world. If you have a favorite verse, I encourage you to take a few moments and ponder what that verse says about you.

My favorite verse in the entire Bible is in this Proverb, so that's what we're going to talk about today! I remember a few years ago when I was reading through Proverbs and this verse leaped off the page at me. I sat there in awe for a few minutes as I stared at the passage, so taken by its words. Over the years, I've been amazed at what the Lord has taught me through it!

> *"Rescue those who are being taken away to death;*
>
> *hold back those who are stumbling to the slaughter.*
>
> *If you say, 'Behold, we did not know this,'*
>
> *does not he who weighs the heart perceive it?*
>
> *Does not he who keeps watch over your soul know it,*
>
> *and will he not repay man according to his work?"*
>
> Proverbs 24:11-12

Honestly, I enjoy swooping in and saving the day. I love fixing problems, and I brim with joy when I'm able to find and implement strategic solutions to make people's lives better. Can you understand why verse 11 gets me all fired up?

We can't rescue others before we are rescued.

I tend to focus on everyone—except me. I get so focused on the task(s) at hand that I neglect myself physically, mentally, emotionally, spiritually, and relationally. My M.O. is to make myself a martyr on the altar of serving others. I think that if I can fix everyone else and all their problems, then I'll be complete in some way. But that's simply not the case. I'm not called to be the end-all be-all rescuer of everyone, and neither are you.

To me, being rescued looks like humbling myself and telling God and other trusted people that I need help. It means choosing to step back from things and say no to people so I'm able to take time for myself. Letting God rescue me looks like pursuing God in good times and bad and submitting to Him regardless of circumstance. It means regularly examining my life for any unhealthy or sinful patterns and putting myself in His hands to heal the things that are broken. I'm no longer allowing myself to cover up my issues by trying to fix others. I'm learning to rest in my identity in Him, rather than trying to find my self-worth in saving other people.

We're not able to save anyone, but we can point others to the One who can.

From what have you been healed? What area is God currently restoring in you? What battles have you overcome?

Those are the areas of authority in your life. The fact that you've walked through illness, lack, doubt, relational breaks, recovery, or any number of other things qualifies you to help those who are still struggling with those things. That's the beautiful power of our stories: they can encourage and empower others to take steps toward Christ.

If you've dealt with substance abuse, you can connect with the person who's still battling a similar issue.

If you've walked through a divorce, you can help others fight that same battle.

If you praise God in the midst of a chronic condition, you will point others to Him.

If you have a strained relationship with a child, you can comfort other grieving parents.

There are so many broken and hurting people in the world today, and we've been given the life, hope, and love they so desperately need. With our stories, we can point people to the Rescuer who can save them from death and provide them with life. We just have to have the eyes to see others and the courage to speak up when the time comes. Our stories of rescue can be the catalyst that pushes them to the Savior.

Reflection

From what have you been rescued?

How are you pointing others to the Rescuer?

What is God saying to you?

DAY 32: PROVERBS 25

Read Proverbs Chapter 25.

What stood out to you in today's Proverb?

I've never prided myself on my performance in social situations. I generally feel awkward when I'm out with other people (unless I know them very well), and crowds are well outside my comfort zone. This leads me to be pretty hyper-aware — a trait that isn't shared by everyone. I'm often stunned by other people's lack of self-awareness! These are the people who stand too close to you in the check-out line, those who linger too long when you're trying to wind down a conversation, and the ones who barge into private moments without batting an eye.

While reading through today's Proverb, I noticed a few social faux pas from which we can learn. I'm amazed that we can still learn about human behavior and relationships from a book that is many centuries old!

The Healing Feeling

What do you do when someone is sad? What do you when you're sad yourself? I'm sure we've all told ourselves, and sometimes even others, "cheer up," or "don't cry," or "there's no reason to be sad." Proverbs 25:20 advises us against exactly that. This verse reminds us that we would be wise to heed the warnings of our emotional intelligence. This feeling of wanting to cheer someone up who's in mourning is well-intentioned but isn't always the most healthy of options. There's something really healthy about being able to express our grief, though it can be incredibly awkward for all parties involved. When we allow ourselves to mourn losses, disappointments, and tragedies, the healing process can begin.

Romans 12:15 is the perfect example of empathy in action: we're to mourn with those who are in mourning instead of singing songs to them to try and cheer them up. While this is a much more uncomfortable way to live, it's amazing how God's presence, comfort, and love can be felt when we quietly sit with a person who's going through a hard time.

Active Spiritual Awareness

Proverbs 25:21-22 takes us from social awareness to spiritual awareness. These verses describe a drastically different way of dealing with enemies—a philosophy that likely would've set readers in Old Testament times reeling. Instead of God raining fire and brimstone down on Israel's enemies, the author is talking about doing something nice for them. The common rhetoric of fighting and battling enemies was replaced with killing them with kindness. When in the presence of someone who has hurt us or those we care about, it's normal to want to get revenge, retribution, or payback, but that's the opposite of what we're instructed to do here. We're supposed to hold ourselves to a higher standard: God's standard. Instead of taking matters into our own hands, we can show kindness to those who have wronged us. After all, we are called to be the hands and feet of Jesus, ambassadors of God whose kindness leads men to repentance.

The mention in Proverbs 25:22 of heaping coals on another's head could be in reference to an ancient Egyptian practice where those who had done something wrong and repented of it would wear hot coals on their heads to show their repentance. Maybe, just maybe, the writer of Proverbs had come to realize the importance God's kindness plays in leading a hurting man or woman to remorse and ultimately, life change.

This is something that's easy to talk about but is much harder to live out. When someone comes around who has hurt me— especially if they've hurt those I care about—I don't want to be nice to them. I want to give them the cold shoulder, I want to gossip about them, I want them to know that I know what they did and I want them to feel bad about it. But that's not what the Bible instructs me to do (even though it might feel good in the moment).

Holding a grudge provides momentary pleasure, but forgiving is a vital part of freedom.

Forgiving is not easy or fun, but it can be the most life-giving thing we do for ourselves and others. Holding on to bitterness and unforgiveness will end up hurting *us* more than anyone else. It's a waste of energy, even though it may feel like the most critical lifeline in the moment. I've been there. Bitterness, hatred, and unforgiveness once fueled me—they were an essential part of my identity. If I didn't have my anger and my chip on my shoulder, I didn't know who I was. But I've been unlearning those past behaviors and choosing to take on new ones instead. I'm learning that I am who God says I am—not who anger and hatred say I should be. I can choose to let go of things just like Jesus tells me to do.

This Proverb challenges us to see social situations around us and respond appropriately. Then the writer goes on to challenge us spiritually by advocating kindness during a time of vengeance. Let's live today with eyes open for those we can empathize with and shower kindness upon, knowing that sometimes the people who need our compassion the most are the ones we least expect.

Reflection

Are you empathetic with others who are having a rough time? How has God shown up in those situations?

Is there anyone you need to forgive? Do you need to repent of any bitterness?

What is God saying to you?

DAY 33: PROVERBS 26

Read Proverbs Chapter 26.

What stood out to you in today's Proverb?

DAY 33: PROVERBS 26

In this Proverb, the writer is back to detailing, in no uncertain terms, what it looks like to be a fool. In example after example, he describes *folly* so we can be on the lookout for it when it comes our way. More than that, these verses serve as a mirror we can hold up to ourselves and ask if we look like the person being described.

The Many Faces of Irresponsibility

"The sluggard says, 'There is a lion in the road!

There is a lion in the streets!'"

Proverbs 26:13

I didn't understand this verse for the longest time. I didn't get how a man warning others of a clear and present danger was a bad thing. His action seems like a good thing to do, not something the writer of Proverbs should be criticizing him for doing.

But when we dig deeper, the real problem becomes obvious: he was crying wolf by crying lion. You see, lions didn't come out during the daytime, but came out of their dens at night. So, if the sluggard was claiming he was unable to go to work because there was a lion in the way, he was flat out lying. He wanted to avoid working so much that he made up an obstacle that prevented him from doing his job. He didn't want to take responsibility for his crummy work ethic but focused instead on this figment of his imagination.

It's effortless for us to avoid accepting responsibility in our lives. It feels like there's always someone or something else to blame for our misfortune. How often do we shift blame to save face in front of someone? Like blaming your assistant in front of your boss, though they did their job well. Or when you blame your spouse for your marital problems or the other party in a friendship tiff. We want to save face to others, sure, but I think the main concern is maintaining a proper view of us, for us.

If I realize that I am irresponsible in a specific area of my life, I'm responsible for handling that accordingly. I can choose to ignore it if I want or I can decide to change, but either way, the onus is on me. If I act like the sluggard, I can continue being ignorant of my irresponsibility.

The Harm of "Just Kidding"

One of my friends used to say, "just kidding!" often. She would say something to someone and, the minute she thought they might not like or receive what she was saying, she would add in that little phrase. For months our group of friends watched her repeat this pattern over and over again, something that had become an unconscious habit for her.

Then, one day, we decided we were going to address this with her. We told her about this pattern and had a moment of real honesty where we spoke life over her. We shared that we would rather she told the truth instead of hiding behind the "just kidding" mask. From that moment on, we began calling her out on this tic whenever she would unconsciously utter the phrase.

That conversation, as hard as it was, was so life-giving for all of us. She was able to dismantle the lie that she would only be liked or accepted if she didn't tell the truth. We were able to love her and be honest with her as she tore down the barrier she had learned to hide behind. We held her accountable and helped her learn that speaking the truth to someone is one of the most loving things you can do for another human being.

We might not have a problem saying "just kidding" to spare the feelings of others, but I'm sure that we all have some belief about how we need to act to be accepted. Maybe it's that we need to help everyone or that we need to be funny or fun all the time. Maybe it's hiding behind a facade of appearance or a career or a cause. And once we don any one of these masks, we begin to believe that a mask removal will lead to instant rejection.

The truth is that some people may drop off if we start to set boundaries, say no, or speak our minds—but I hope we will be able to identify the people who will be with us no matter what. They're the ones we don't have to put on a mask to impress, but those we can be ourselves around.

While going through Proverbs, I'm learning that folly can be oh so subtle. Even the wisest and most mature of us can have veins of foolish thinking running through our minds that the Lord wants to root out. He wants to erase the lies we've believed that have led to foolish behaviors. Every day is an opportunity to follow Jesus a little closer, leaving foolish ways behind and listening to wisdom instead.

Reflection

Are there any current areas of irresponsibility in your life?

What facades do you hide behind in the hopes that people will accept you?

What is God saying to you?

DAY 34: PROVERBS 27

Read Proverbs Chapter 27.

What stood out to you in today's Proverb?

I'm learning that I'm a selectively-opinionated person. I'm very opinionated about things like art and politics, but I have little opinion on things like food or clothing. I hadn't realized this about myself until I noticed a trend of people coming to me and asking what I thought of things. Books, movies, ideas, business plans, decisions, politics, and more — it's all fair game with me.

Because of this, I've been more aware of what I call "good." There are certain movies or books I'll deem "good" because of the quality of the work that is produced, while the content might not be morally good. I might consider a business idea "good" in that it is effective and revenue generating, while it might not be the best decision for that particular person to make. I might call a political decision "good" when in reality, it's merely the lesser of two evils.

What do you call "good" and how do you arrive at that conclusion?

"The crucible is for silver, and the furnace is for gold,

and a man is tested by his praise."

Proverbs 27:21

This verse stood out to me when I read it. I felt like I couldn't get away from it. Once again, our hearts are so clearly linked to the words we say, specifically the things we celebrate.

The truth is that my speech isn't always what it should be. My admiration isn't always directed toward things that are truly good and worthy of praise. Often I get caught up in focusing on things that are less than praiseworthy and forget to celebrate that which is honorable, noble, pure, or wonderful.

Just like so many other Proverbs have done, I am once again reminded of the fact that my affections are still out of order. My speech has given me away again.

Years ago, my go-to response would've been a speech modification plan. I would stop saying certain words, stop taking in specific media, delete particular podcasts from my queue, and eliminate anything that might tempt me to call something that's not good, "good." But now, I don't think that's the right solution. I don't think there's anything wrong with setting boundaries for myself in what I take in, but since my speech reveals the state of my heart, I have to focus on changing my heart before changing my speech. If I change my affections, my speech will change as a natural byproduct.

The best way I've found to change my heart is by changing how I spend my time. When I spend more time thinking about the goodness of God, I fall more in love with Him. When I read His Word — His love letter written to humanity — I can't help but desire to spend more time with Him. When I speak to people who are passionate about God and listen to sermons declaring His glory, I can't help but celebrate Him. When I have Him regularly at the forefront of my mind, my affections have no choice but to follow suit.

As Christians, those who know the goodness, purity, love, and righteousness of God, we should be experts on what is "good." When we say something is "good," "right," "true," "noble," or "pure," that should hold some extra weight because we know the standard for these qualities. Unfortunately, I often call things "good" that don't look like God and if they don't look like God, they can't possibly be good.

Today, I encourage you to take a closer look at what you praise. What do you call good or great? What do you label as awesome or amazing? I would imagine that many of these words come out of our mouths without much thought, some of which are most definitely not fitting. When we see someone fall physically or metaphorically and we think, *good*. Or the moment when something bad happens and we exclaim, "Well, isn't that just great!" Or when we call something detrimental to ourselves "good," revealing the true state of our hearts.

I imagine that as we monitor our language a little more closely, the Lord will begin to illuminate parts of our hearts and minds that He longs to heal. Let's choose to start this lifelong examination process today!

Reflection

What do you call "good?" What are your criteria for goodness?

What does your speech reveal about your affections?

What is God saying to you?

DAY 35: PROVERBS 28

Read Proverbs Chapter 28.

What stood out to you in today's Proverb?

I absolutely despise injustice. The face of it doesn't matter in my mind — human trafficking, poverty, education inequality, criminal justice violations, or a hundred other things — I *hate* injustice. If a group of people, a policy, or a practice hurts a person or a group of people, I get angry and, more than that, I want to expend all of my energy to fix the problem.

Justice is one of those concepts that many people define differently. According to many Americans, justice looks like retribution: if you commit a crime, if you harm someone else, you have to pay an equal payment. There has to be some form of restitution. But that's not always how it works with God. This Proverb tells us that we should understand justice completely because we are in a relationship with the one who is Just. Justice isn't a judge in a big black robe, sitting behind a formidable desk and banging a gavel to decree his or her order.

True justice looks like Jesus.

Jesus's life, death, and resurrection are the perfect image of justice — in addition to being the personification of love. And the more we pursue God, the more time we spend with the One who made us and saved us, the more we'll understand what justice truly is. Have you ever taken a moment to think about the injustice Jesus encountered when He walked the earth?

If you had a disease, you were an outcast.

The religious leaders were corrupt thieves.

The Roman government oppressed people.

Righting Religious Injustice

One of my favorite stories of Jesus in the Bible is found in Matthew 21, where Jesus overturns the tables in the temple. As much as I love the image of Hulk-Jesus, I love what it says about who God is.

In the Jewish culture, the men of each family had to come to the temple with some regularity to offer a sacrifice to atone for their family's sin. Poor people would show up with an animal, but the religious leaders could reject the animal, saying it wasn't "up to code," forcing the already poor person to buy a "Temple Approved" version so they could atone for their sins. The religious guys would then take the animal they had just labeled "unacceptable" and use it to sell to the next guy that came by, making profits off the sacrifices of the people.

This was a clear case of injustice that Jesus sought to remedy. After He turned over the tables, the blind and lame people entered the temple to be healed by Him because they were no longer barred from entry. Justice prevailed that day: people were healed, their relationships with God were restored, and they learned just how loved they were.

Paying Back Ill-Gotten Gains

Zacchaeus is an interesting Bible character who has a very irritating children's song attributed to his name. In fact, that song is playing in my head right now and, if that's happening to you right now, I'm sorry.

This man was a tax collector whose job was to collect taxes from Jewish people that he then passed on to the Roman government. However, tax collectors were notorious for profiting off of others, their own people, by collecting more taxes than were actually owed. Zacchaeus was no exception to this and he amassed a considerable fortune during this time.

But when he met Jesus, everything changed.

As a result of his new faith in Christ, he agreed to give half of his possessions to the poor and promised to pay back four times what he stole from others! (That's some incredible life change!) True justice isn't an outward behavior but originates from the heart.

Restoring a Stolen Identity

One of my favorite Bible stories is the healing of the woman with the issue of blood. Because of her disease, she had almost everything taken from her: her identity, her relationships, her faith, and more. This was as a result of a religious law that was no longer applicable once Jesus came onto the scene.

In that second, when Jesus called her "daughter" in front of the crowd, commended her faith, and declared her healthy and whole —justice was restored. What had been taken from her, the names she had been called, and the isolation she endured, were all made right in that second.

The more time we spend with Jesus, the more we'll know what justice looks like because He is justice. Not only did He come to bring justice for all of us in a macro sense, He also came to bring justice to individuals. I used to believe that justice was filled with harshness, punishment, and penalties, but now I know better.

Now I'm confident that justice looks like Jesus.

Reflection

What does justice mean to you?

Do you think justice looks like Jesus? Why or why not?

What is God saying to you?

DAY 36: PROVERBS 29

Read Proverbs Chapter 29.

What stood out to you in today's Proverb?

Nothing happens in a vacuum.

This is one of my favorite phrases because it means that nothing happens independently of everything else around it. My life isn't a series of isolated, compartmentalized decisions, but is a result of interconnected events, thoughts, beliefs, motivations, and actions. Even if I don't like to admit it, my relationships affect my work which influences my mental state which affects my body which impacts what I do and how I live. Everything I do is related to everything else I do.

Today's Proverb reminds us that we're all connected and profoundly influence one another: the decisions I make and the interactions I have impact the lives of others in little and big ways. One kind word to one person might change the trajectory of their day. And my grumpy mood in the office might bring everyone down, even if that's not my intention.

This chapter reminds us that people who know God interact with society in a different way than people who don't know God. The writer contrasts the acts of these two groups and how others respond to them, and they couldn't be more different.

The Righteous Handle Trials Differently

Have you ever been around a person who was having a rough time and took it out on everyone else? Me too! And I've been that person on more than one occasion. It's incredible how much our moods can influence the people around us.

Now, when I say we respond differently, I am by no means suggesting that we should detach from our emotions or numb ourselves in certain situations. What I do mean is that we hold a different perspective that automatically changes our response. When we know and trust God above all else, we can go through hard times without being crushed. We can still praise God in the midst of an intense battle and point people to Him in the middle of difficulty.

Will we do this perfectly every (or any) time? Of course not! But we have a hope that can help us endure through even the craziest of seasons.

The Righteous Treat the Poor Well

Honor can be an awkward topic of conversation depending on the context, but I think that has to do with a misconception of what honor is. I used to think I only had to respect or honor people who were in power or those who had some level of influence, but that's just not the case. We are called to treat others well, to respect those around us, and to honor even those who are different than us, simply because they're human beings.

People who are pursuing God understand that loving others the way God loves isn't conditional. This is easy to talk about and a lot harder to live out—but that doesn't make it any less true.

The Righteous are Careful with Their Words

This is a theme throughout the Bible and especially in the book of Proverbs, so we're going to hit on it yet again. In this chapter, the difference between the speech of the righteous and the speech of the wicked is obvious. No wonder people rejoice when the righteous increase—look how they talk and interact with others!

What's comforting to me about this is that we're righteous because of Jesus when we accept His life instead of living on our own terms. In an instant, our status goes from "unrighteous" to "righteous," with no work on our part. And even after we're declared "righteous," the changing of our behavior to conform to our new state isn't entirely dependent upon us.

We don't have to strive or muscle out this new way of living. Instead, it flows naturally from us as we draw nearer to Him on a daily basis. The more time we spend with Him, the more we'll react to trials, interact with the poor, and use our words like He does — which will be to the praise of everyone around us!

Reflection

How do you handle trials? Treat the poor? Use your words?

What's one area you can be more intentional about today?

What is God saying to you?

DAY 37: PROVERBS 30

Read Proverbs Chapter 30.

What stood out to you in today's Proverb?

I enjoy researching. When I read a book or watch a movie, I want to know all about the people who created the work and what caused them to make the choices they did. Context is immensely important to me, so seeing how a project fits within the person's life can help me better understand and appreciate the creative work I'm experiencing. Factors like time period, where it was written, who it was written to, and what purpose the work served all play significant roles in illuminating the work as a whole. It's incredible how the same words written to one group of people can carry a different meaning in a different context.

Proverbs 30 raises many questions for me as I read it. Proverbs 30:1 tells us that these words were written by a man named Agur, son of Jakeh. I really appreciate that he gets that out of the way right off the bat! Armed with his name, I set off on a searching spree to find out more information about this elusive author, but my searching came up relatively empty.

At first, I was annoyed by this. I wanted an answer because I love figuring things out. I wanted to be able to wow you with my researching skills. I longed to be able to share something with you that you didn't know before. But then my perspective changed.

I realized that finding out information about this writer wasn't the most important thing. In fact, if there's little known about this guy, that's probably for a strategic reason. If God wanted us to know about this author, He would've dished all the dirt on him. But He didn't. Instead, we only have this isolated chapter.

What a beautiful picture of how the Lord works!

Contrary to the messaging found throughout social media, most of us will never become famous. Our names won't be found in lights, we won't be on the big screen, we won't command the attention of millions or billions at a time—and that's okay. Many of us will only be known by a few hundred people at most. The majority of us will have a direct impact on select groups of people like family, friends, coworkers, and church family, with little effect outside of that. But that isn't a bad thing. It just makes us like Agur.

This truth is so comforting to me! I don't have to be famous, on a stage or television, or the leader of a Fortune 500 Company to make a difference in the world. I just have to be me! I have to use the gifts and the opportunities that God has entrusted to me for His glory and the good of others. I can choose to leave a legacy using what's right in front of me. After all, little by little, we are trusted with more.

The truth is that day by day and minute by minute we're building a legacy. We're compiling attitudes, words, projects, products, relationships, worldviews, and more that influence how we interact with the world around us. The things we say, the time we invest in others, the works we create, and the way we live will outlast us—even though we often forget this important fact.

Every day we're presented with the opportunity to build something that's going to outlast us.

What Legacy Are You Leaving?

Centuries after his death, Agur is still known and his words are still being read. Though little else is known about him, he is recognized for his wisdom and his incredible example to others. That sounds like a pretty good legacy to me!

This chapter reminds me of the truth that what we do for God remains, even long after we're gone. The wealth we amass or don't, the things we create or don't, the things we consume or don't aren't going to last—but the way we interact with people, the righteousness we display in our lives, and the wisdom we exercise will outlast us.

Agur reminds me that the goal for our lives doesn't have to be a certain number of followers, a certain amount in the bank, or a certain level of notoriety. The goal should be to love God and love people, which is the wisest thing we can do!

Reflection

What legacy do you want to leave?

What's one thing you can do to positively impact those in your sphere of influence today?

What is God saying to you?

DAY 38: PROVERBS 30

Read Proverbs Chapter 30.

What stood out to you in today's Proverb?

You read that right — we're still in Proverbs 30 today! Honestly, it's such a good chapter, and I wasn't ready to move on from it just yet!

There are so many ways to view God and, for many years, I saw Him incorrectly. At first, I thought He was mean — a harsh authoritarian who relished in punishing me. Then I thought He was like a genie or Santa Claus who had to respond to my good deeds reciprocally. But that's not at all who He is. God is a good Father who loves His children and longs to give us good gifts. He doesn't always give us what we want but, when we learn His character, we can trust His actions, despite how circumstances appear.

What I've found is that my requests of God have changed over the years as my view of Him has changed. When I thought God was mean, I didn't ever ask Him for things because I didn't think He'd ever give them to me. I wanted nothing to do with Him and assumed He wanted nothing to do with me. When I thought God was a transaction-based being, I felt I had to come to Him when I met specific requirements and, when those were met, I expected something in return. Now, because we're in a relationship, I'm learning to come to God with every little thing (though some days this is easier than others).

If you could only ask God for one thing, what would it be?

It's a seriously hard question to answer, *right*? World peace? A global ceasefire? Injustice to end? A million dollars? Your health to be restored? A relationship to be healed? There are many different answers to this question, and each one reveals something about the heart. When Solomon was asked this question, he had a brilliant answer locked and loaded: *wisdom*. And God was perfectly happy fulfilling that request and much, much more.

If you could ask God for two things, what would they be?

Another Proverbs writer named Agur, son of Jakeh, gives us his answer in this Proverb. We know very little about this man. We don't even know when this particular Proverb was written. But we do know this: the Holy Spirit inspired it.

In Proverbs 30:7-9, the writer shares his two requests of God.

1. To remove lying from him.
2. To give only what's needed for him—no more, no less.

I don't know about you, but that's definitely not what would be on my list. My jaw dropped when I read through these verses. I needed to camp out here for a few moments. Agur knew the heart of God so much that he didn't want anything in his mind, heart, or life that would potentially separate him from the God who loved him!

I'm amazed at how different my value systems are in this regard. I love the Lord deeply and I desire to do His will but there are many things I want to keep in my life, even though I know I should cut them out. Often I value my comfort over all else and I want things done my way. I can get so caught up in my thoughts, life, work, and desires that I let the things of God fall by the wayside. At times, I will do all that's in my power to get ahead and I will hoard things, finding my identity in what I possess. Lord, heal my heart!

This chapter is a brilliant crescendo of what it looks like to fully pursue God.

Throughout Proverbs, God's hatred of falsehood and lying are stated in no uncertain terms. His feelings about inaccurate scales are clear and His heart for people shines through the entire book. It only makes sense for God to hate the things that run so contrary to His character — traits that shouldn't characterize His children. Knowing this truth, Agur longed for the things that pain God to be removed from his mouth, heart, and presence. He didn't want anything to drive a wedge between him and his God.

Then, as if the lying thing wasn't enough, he asked for neither poverty nor riches — only what he needed for that day. He didn't want to fall into the ditch on either side of the money conversation. He didn't want to risk finding his identity in either poverty or opulence. He wasn't concerned about the needs for tomorrow because he knew that today had enough problems.

The truth is that we're so much more than the things we have — we're children of God! Our identities aren't based on our possessions but on our position. Agur understood this. He didn't want to get greedy and develop a big head, nor did he want to fall into the poverty mindset. Instead, he trusted God so much that he asked for only what he needed, not a penny more or a penny less.

The good news is that we don't develop these wants all on our own — they're a result of a relationship with the Lord. Though lying and materialism are rampant today and deeply ingrained in our sinful nature, we can overcome them through the cross.

Because of Christ, we can choose to live a different way, pursuing God openly and honestly, finding our identities fully in Him. And when we mess up (as we will inevitably do) we can run back to the cross and seek refuge in His arms! I encourage you to run to Him today!

Reflection

If you could ask God for two things what would they be?

Do your prayers look like Agur's? I encourage you to pray verses 7-9 this week and see what happens in your heart.

What is God saying to you?

DAY 39: PROVERBS 31

Read Proverbs Chapter 31.

What stood out to you in today's Proverb?

Proverbs 31 is one of those chapters of the Bible that has typically been geared toward women. It seems like the Proverbs 31 Woman is mentioned at every women's conference, in Christian books directed toward women, and all over timelines and feeds of middle-aged moms. Ministries have been named after her and women strive to be like her, but I believe there's so much more to this chapter.

This woman was described over and over again to King Lemuel by his mother. She wanted him to find a good woman to be his wife, sure, but I believe she also wanted him to be a good man, *worthy* of "Mrs. Right." I imagine his mother knew that if you want a partner who is trustworthy, you also need to be trustworthy. If you're going to be with someone who is respected, you need to give respect. If you want to be with someone who follows God with all their heart, you need to also be fully yielded to God.

We've made Proverbs 31 all about this incredible woman, but have forgotten about the amazing man to whom she was married! Instead of focusing on the revered woman in the story, I want to take a look at her husband.

Meet The Proverbs 31 Man

"An excellent wife who can find? She is far more precious than jewels.

The heart of her husband trusts in her, and he will have no lack of gain."

Proverbs 31:10-11

"Her husband is known in the gates when he sits among

the elders of the land."

Proverbs 31:23

"Her children rise up and call her blessed; her husband also,

and he praises her:

'Many women have done excellently, but you surpass them all.'"

Proverbs 31:28-29

I am in awe of the man described in these few verses. Right off the bat, we learn that he trusts his wife and has empowered her to make decisions and run the household—and his trust isn't misplaced. He has entrusted her with more and more and more over the years because she was a good steward. What a beautiful cycle of trust and respect exchanged between these two!

His life and speech were characterized by honor—he respected God, his family, and his elders. He spoke well of his wife in public and in private. And his honor wasn't a façade—it permeated his every action. Have you ever taken a moment to think about how rare that must've been during that time in history?

She was entrepreneurial, and he respected that. He gave her the space to pursue her business and craft while he did his job. He honored her ability to make money and her desire for more. He could humbly step aside and allow her to take the reins on some things. He wasn't intimidated by his wife's competency but encouraged her in that.

Complimentary Relationships

The Proverbs 31 Man and Woman were complementary partners for one another. To use a Bible term, these two were equally yoked. My question for us is this: Who are you yoked to? And do they complement you?

If you want a friend, spouse, or business partner to be honoring, trustworthy, and kind—first, ask yourself if you're those things. It's so easy to focus on other people and all that they aren't, blaming them for not living up to our standards. If you do this, there's no judgment here. I was a pro at this move. But I'm learning that there's a better way.

If I want to be around generous people, I have to work on my generosity. If I want to be around people who are joyful, I have to reassess my joy source. If I long for transparency in all areas, I need to also be transparent.

No matter your age or current relationship status, I believe we can all become like the man and woman described in Proverbs 31. Let's trust, respect, and love others to the best of our ability and watch the cycle of reciprocity begin!

Reflection

Do you relate to the couple Proverbs 31 mentions? Why or why not?

How can you be intentional to trust, respect, and love others this week?

What is God saying to you?

DAY 40: A SUMMARY

Wow, we did it! We've made it to the 40th day and all the way through the book of Proverbs!

Thank you for walking with me through this amazing book for the last few weeks. It's been an honor to journey with you!

We've spent time discussing the importance of wisdom and the perils of folly, the heart of God and His desire for our hearts and minds, and some ways to practically change our thoughts and behaviors.

So, to close out our time together, I have two questions to ask:

1. How has your view of God changed over the last 40 days?

2. How has your view of yourself changed over the last 40 days?

We might have many, *many* loves and desires but God loves and desires you. You're His favorite, and He is passionately pursuing you. I hope you've seen a glimpse of that over the past few weeks and that you've experienced His presence in a more tangible way than you ever have before.

Today we're going to keep it short so you can have a few extra moments to pray and reflect on what God has done in your life over the last 40 days. Take some time to write out what you're grateful for and praise God for the little and big ways you've seen Him move in your life.

And know this: I'm so proud of you for passionately pursuing God! I can't wait to see how He continues to show up on your behalf in the coming weeks, months, and years.

Final Reflection

Today, I'm thankful for...

I used to believe _____ about God.

Now I believe _____.

I used to believe _____ about myself.

Now I believe _____.

What is God saying to you?

ABOUT THE AUTHOR

Sarah J Callen is an entrepreneur and published author, currently living in Dallas, Texas. She is passionate about creating safe spaces with people where honest conversations about life and faith can occur. Her dreams include founding businesses, giving strategically, and sharing art with the world.

Her life motto is: Every number has a name, every name has a story, and every story is worthy of being shared.

You can connect with her on her website, sarahjcallen.com or on social media @sarahjcallen.

Made in United States
Orlando, FL
11 July 2022

19624389R00148